スター・ウォーズ

新たなる希望
〈下〉

"WHERE DO YOU THINK YOU'RE GOING?"

STAR WARS: A NEW HOPE — MANGA is a translation which was first published in Japan by Media Works. In Japan, manga is normally read from right-to-left. In order to conform to Western standards, the art in this book was copied in a mirror-image to facilitate left-to-right reading of the pages. This, of course, can cause some confusion in a story such as STAR WARS: A NEW HOPE — MANGA where readers are somewhat familiar with the material and so will notice characters both moving and appearing in an opposite fashion from that which they did in the film. We apologize for any confusion this may cause and hope that it will not detract from your enjoyment of this volume.

ピキュー
ピ
いいか もう私を当てにするなよ 絶対に助けてやらないからな
これ以上わけのわからないことに巻き込まれるのはもうごめんだよ！

WHAT MISSION? WHAT ARE YOU TALKING ABOUT?
I'VE JUST ABOUT HAD ENOUGH OF YOU! GO THAT WAY!
YOU'LL BE MAL-FUNCTIONING WITHIN A DAY, YOU NEARSIGHTED SCRAP PILE!
VEE-BEE! BOOP!

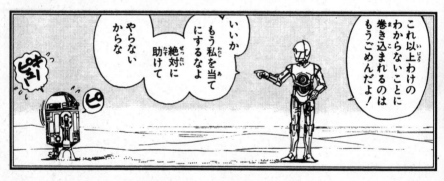

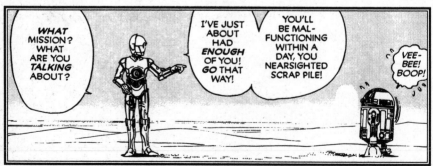

A long time ago in a galaxy far, far away....

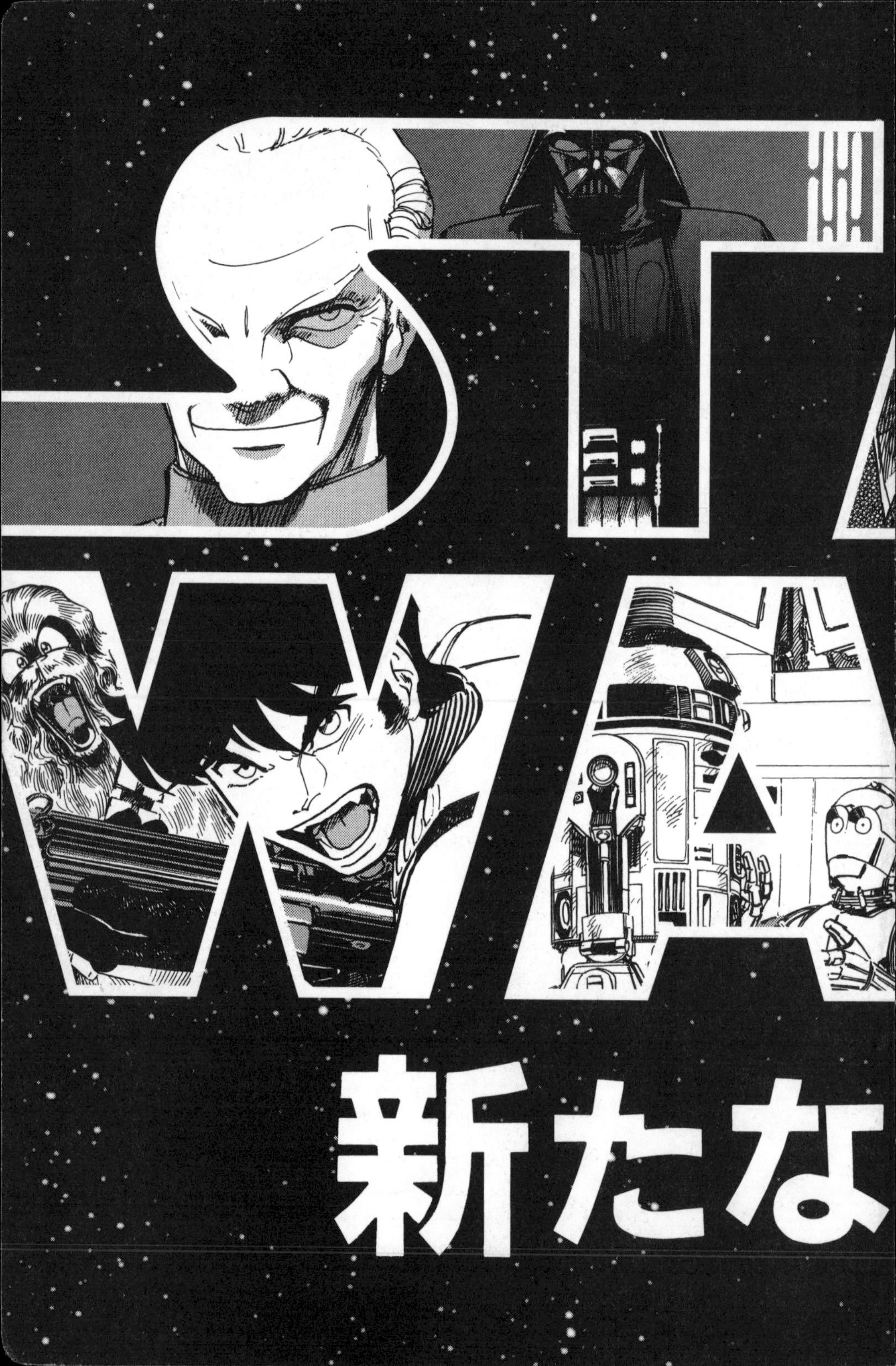
新たな

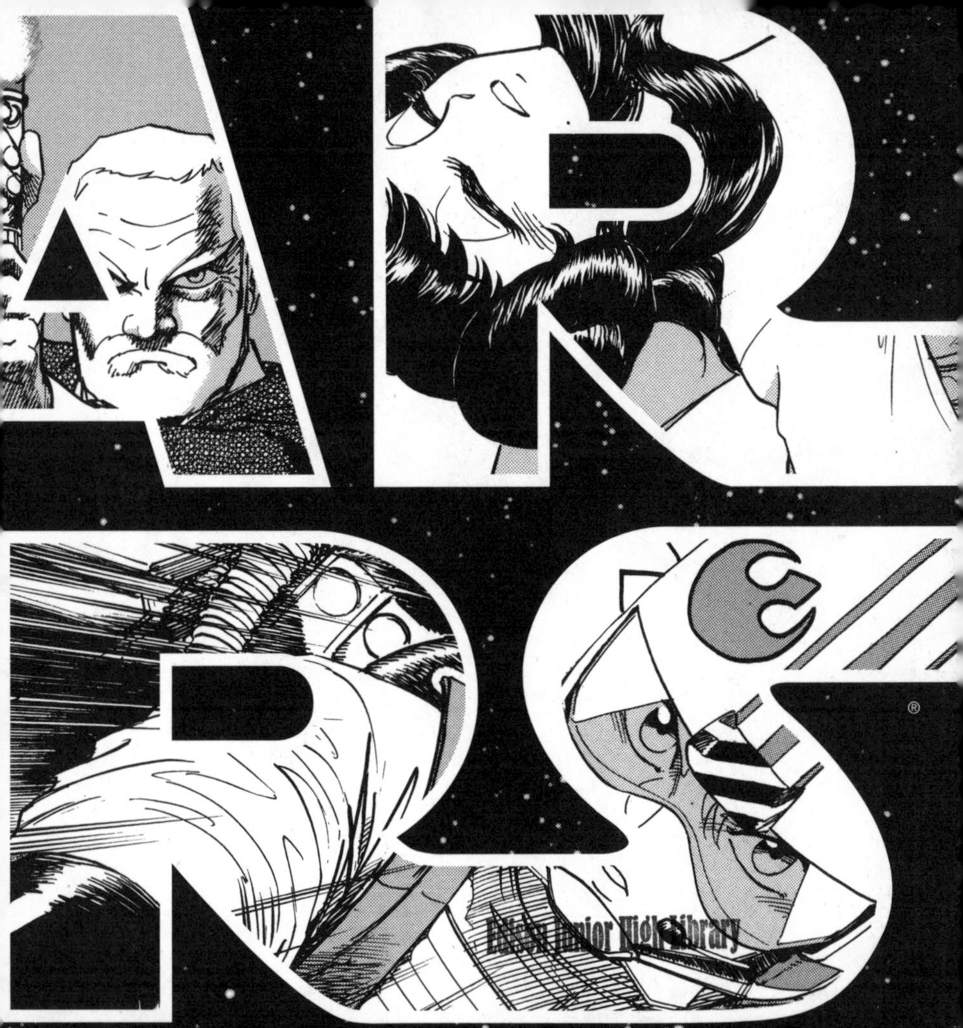
AR
RS
®

る希望

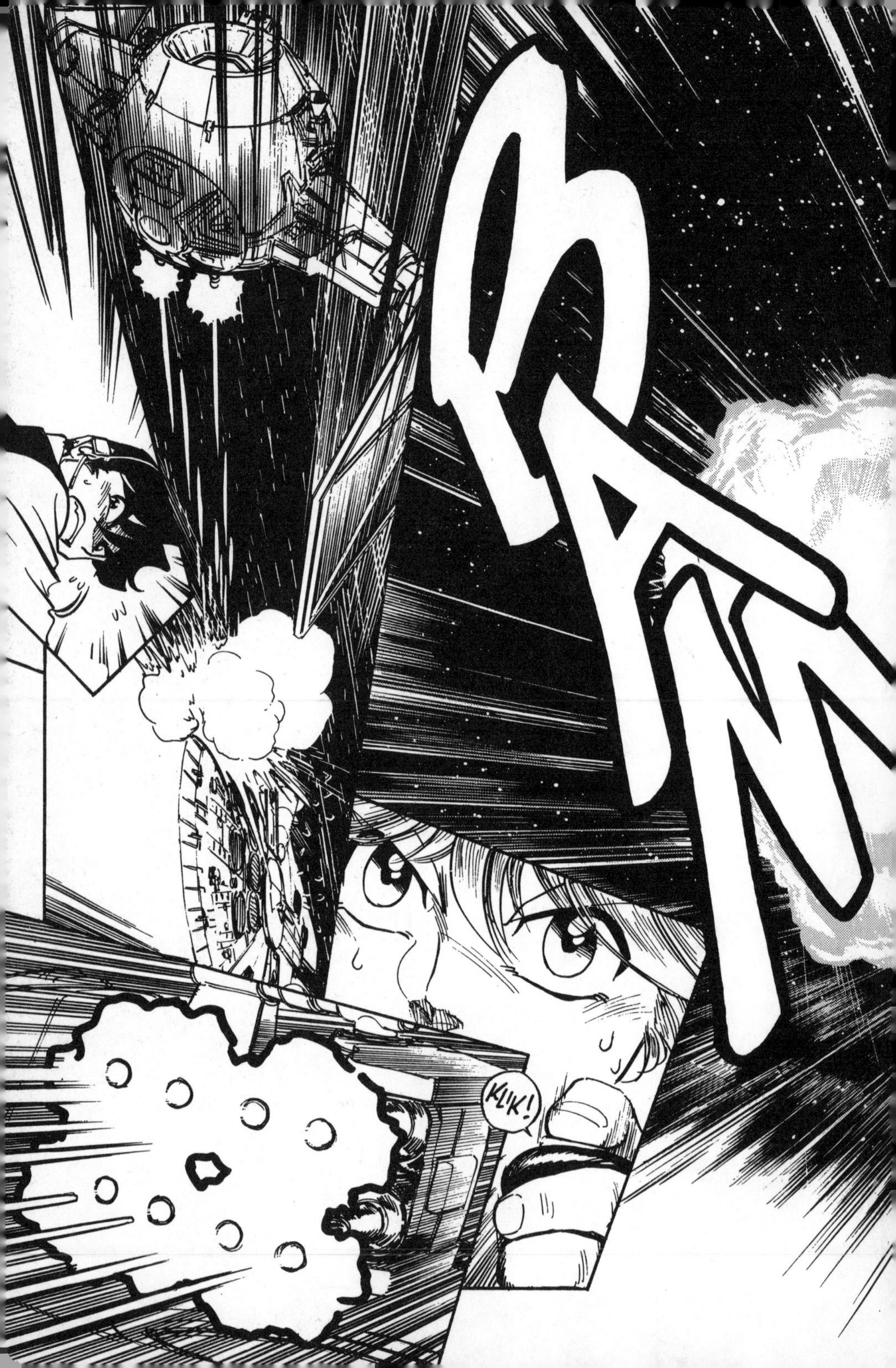
BAM
KLIK!

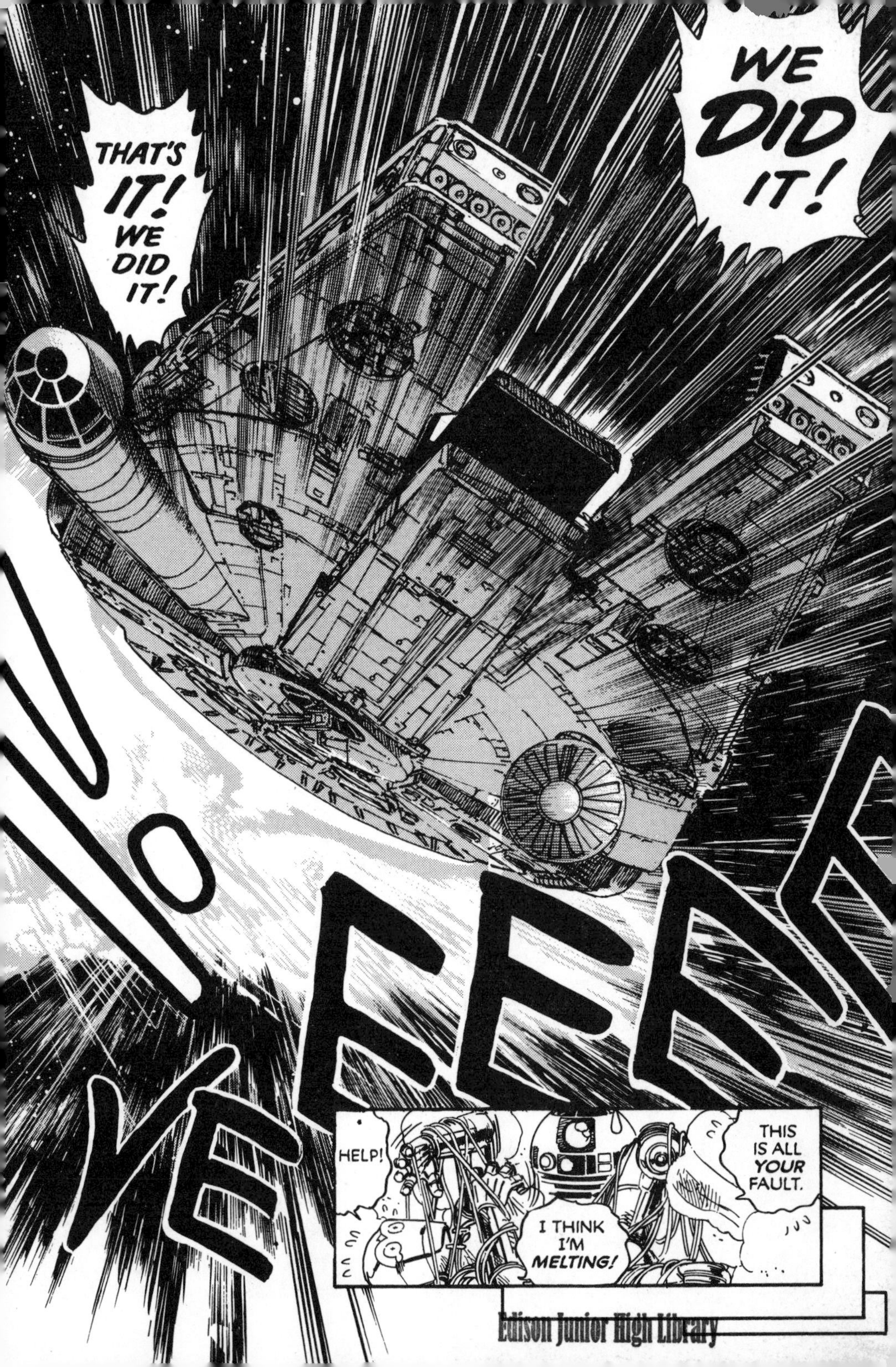

THAT'S IT! WE DID IT!
WE DID IT!
YEEE
HELP!
THIS IS ALL YOUR FAULT.
I THINK I'M MELTING!

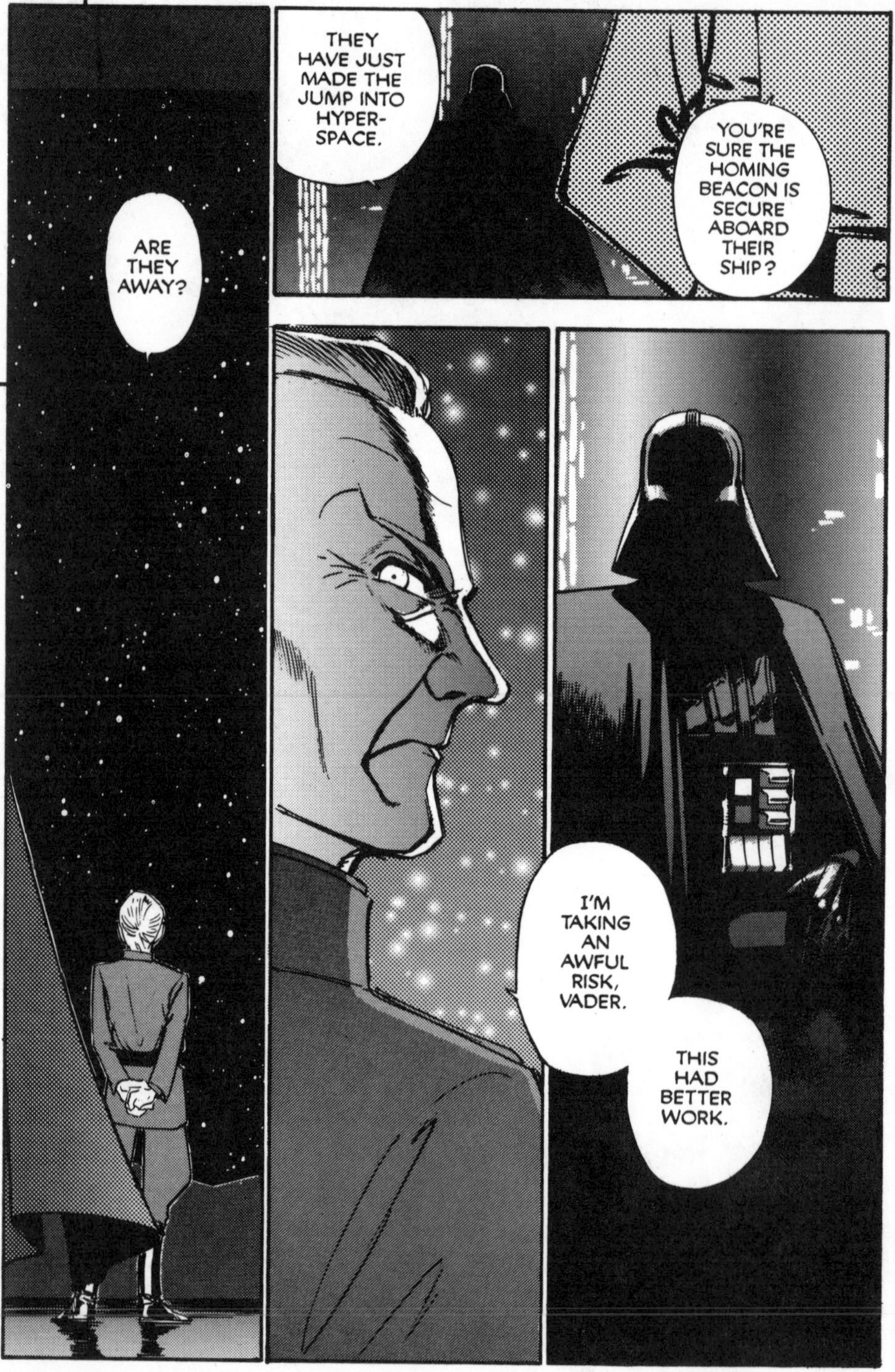
ARE THEY AWAY?
THEY HAVE JUST MADE THE JUMP INTO HYPER-SPACE.
YOU'RE SURE THE HOMING BEACON IS SECURE ABOARD THEIR SHIP?
I'M TAKING AN AWFUL RISK, VADER.
THIS HAD BETTER WORK.

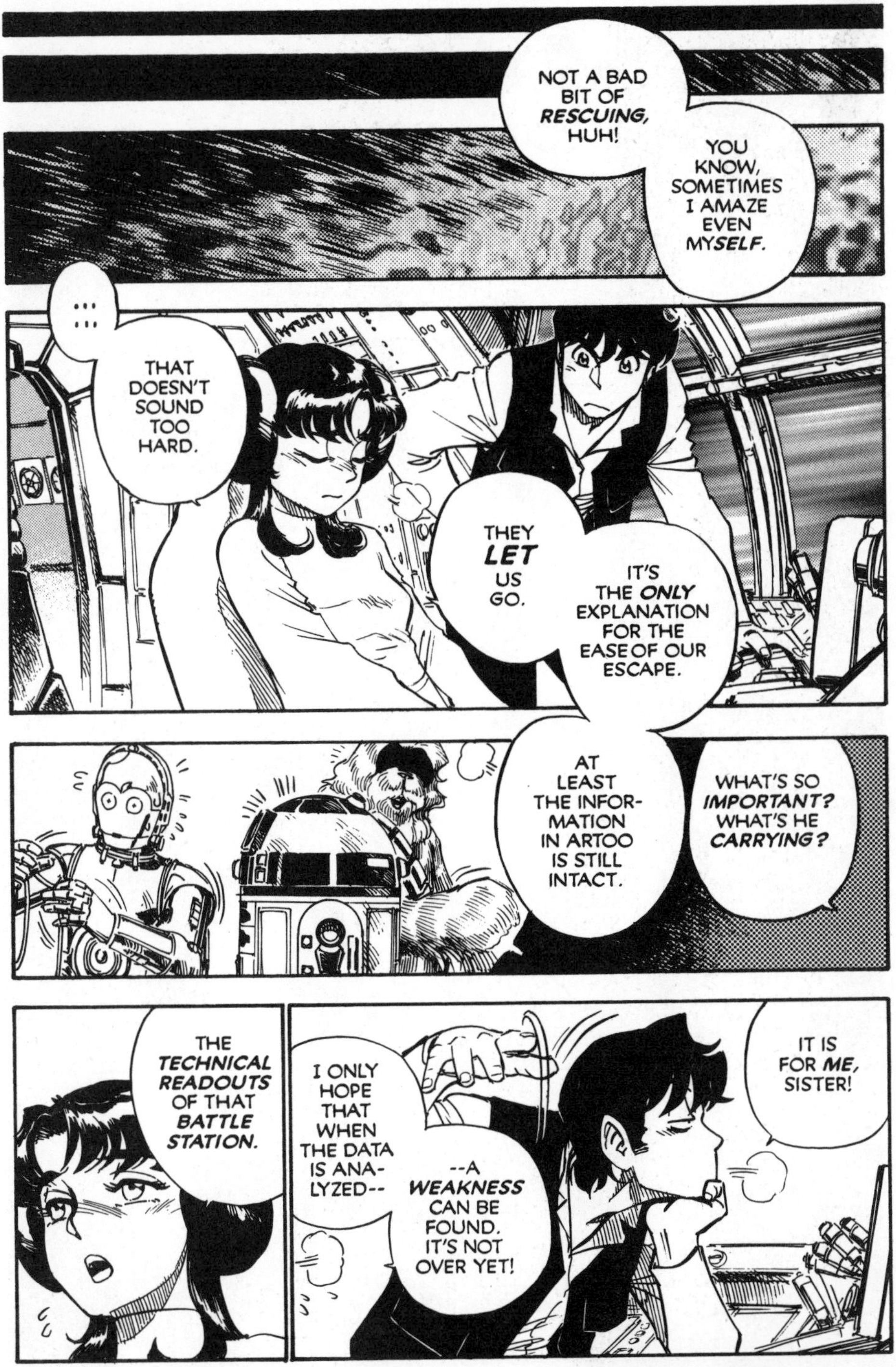
NOT A BAD BIT OF RESCUING, HUH!
YOU KNOW, SOMETIMES I AMAZE EVEN MYSELF.
...
THAT DOESN'T SOUND TOO HARD.
THEY LET US GO.
IT'S THE ONLY EXPLANATION FOR THE EASE OF OUR ESCAPE.
AT LEAST THE INFOR-MATION IN ARTOO IS STILL INTACT.
WHAT'S SO IMPORTANT? WHAT'S HE CARRYING?
THE TECHNICAL READOUTS OF THAT BATTLE STATION.
I ONLY HOPE THAT WHEN THE DATA IS ANA-LYZED--
--A WEAKNESS CAN BE FOUND. IT'S NOT OVER YET!
IT IS FOR ME, SISTER!

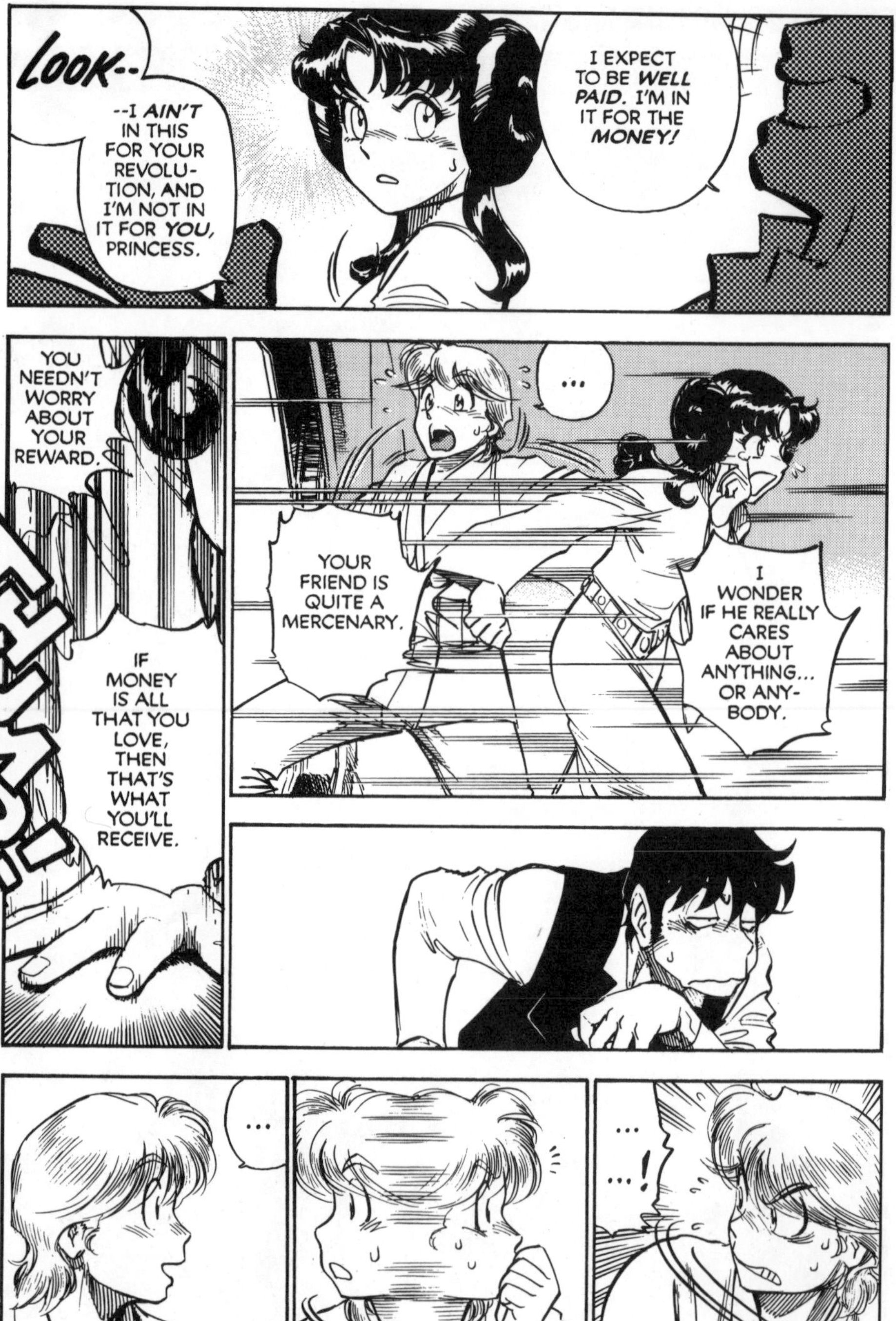
LOOK--
--I AIN'T IN THIS FOR YOUR REVOLUTION, AND I'M NOT IN IT FOR YOU, PRINCESS.
I EXPECT TO BE WELL PAID. I'M IN IT FOR THE MONEY!
YOU NEEDN'T WORRY ABOUT YOUR REWARD.
IF MONEY IS ALL THAT YOU LOVE, THEN THAT'S WHAT YOU'LL RECEIVE.
THWAP!
...
YOUR FRIEND IS QUITE A MERCENARY.
I WONDER IF HE REALLY CARES ABOUT ANYTHING... OR ANYBODY.
...
...
...!

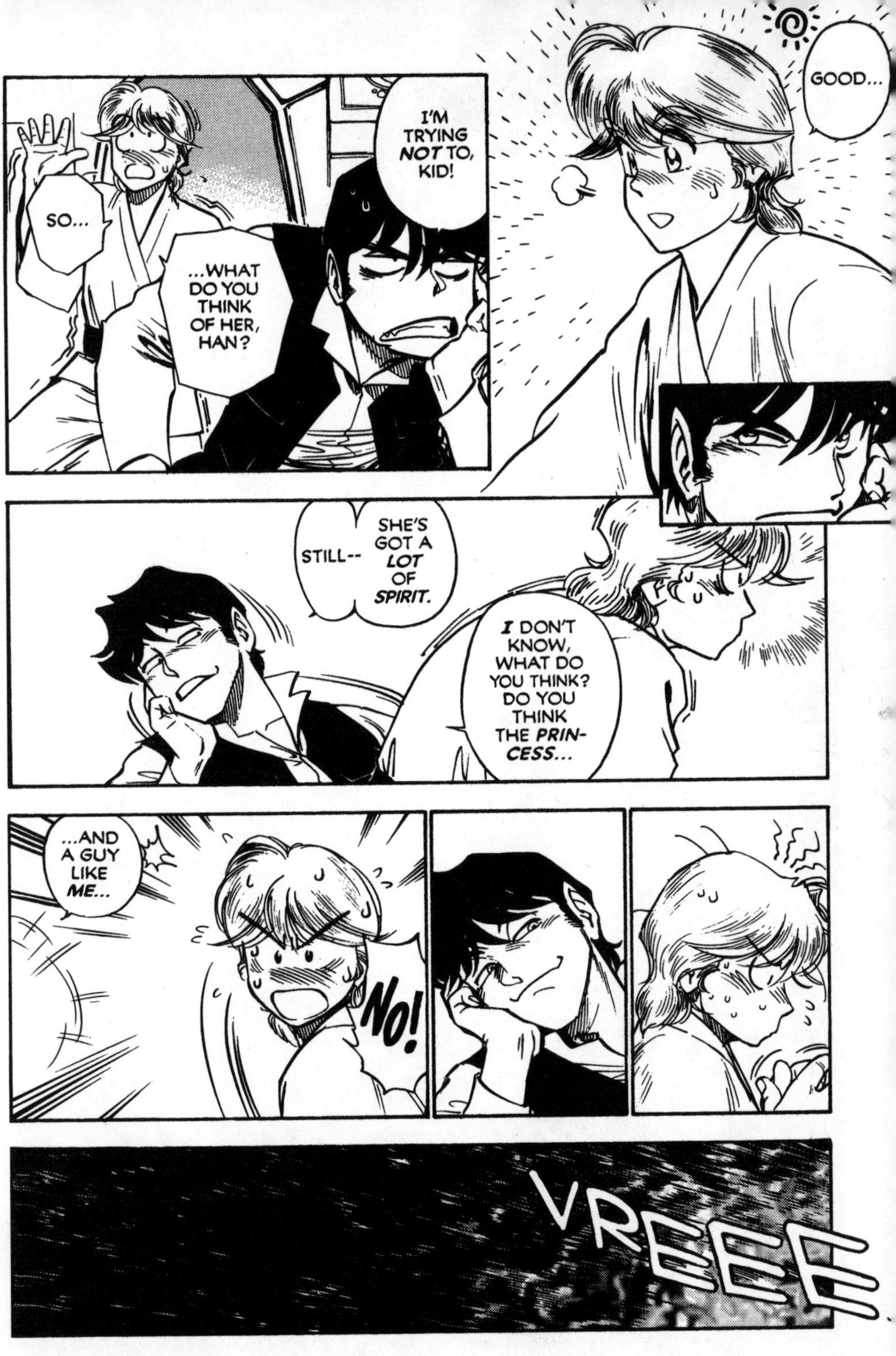
SO...
...WHAT DO YOU THINK OF HER, HAN?
I'M TRYING NOT TO, KID!
GOOD...
STILL--
SHE'S GOT A LOT OF SPIRIT.
I DON'T KNOW, WHAT DO YOU THINK? DO YOU THINK THE PRINCESS...
...AND A GUY LIKE ME...
NO!
VREEEE

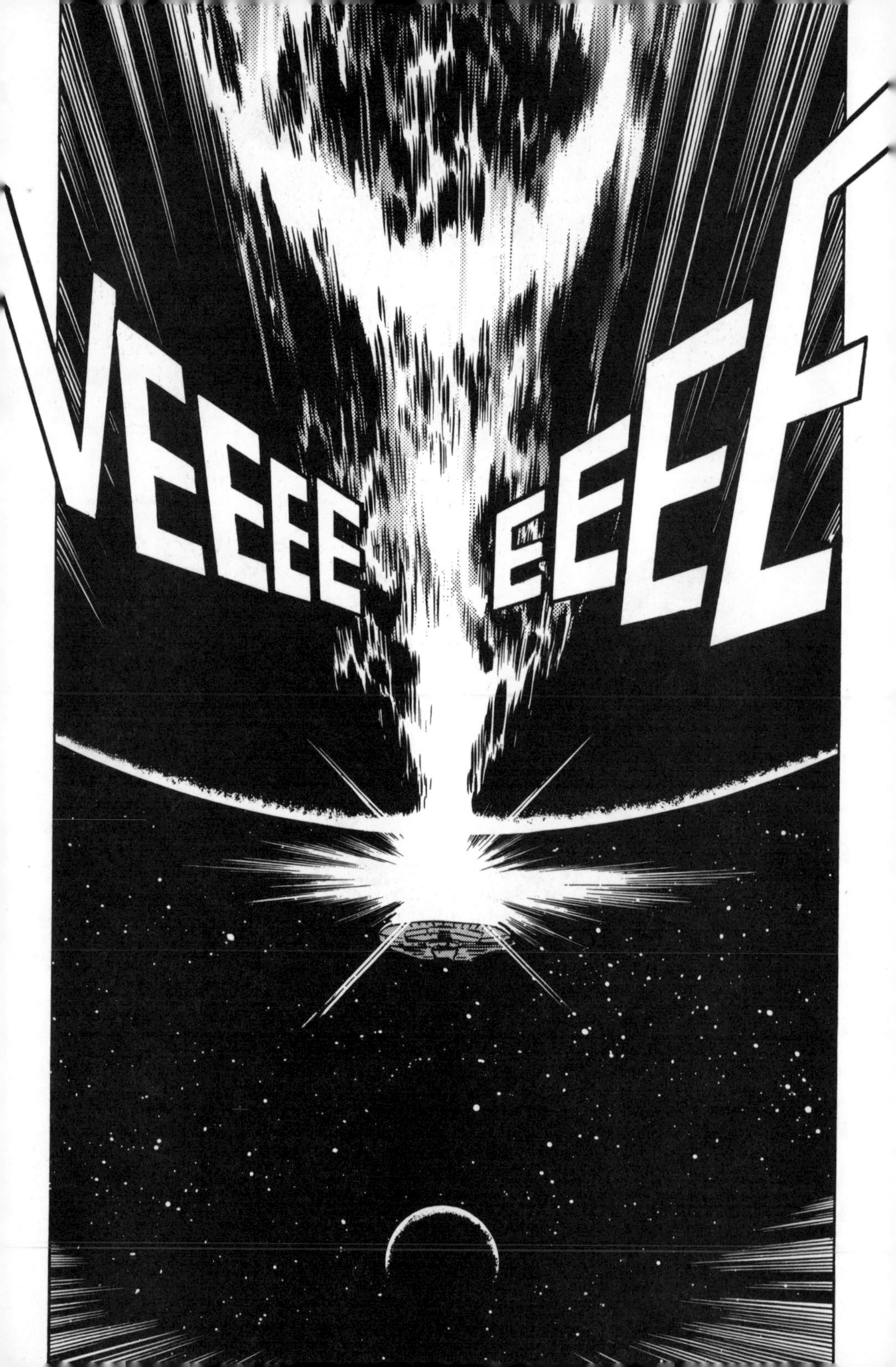
VEEEEEEEEE

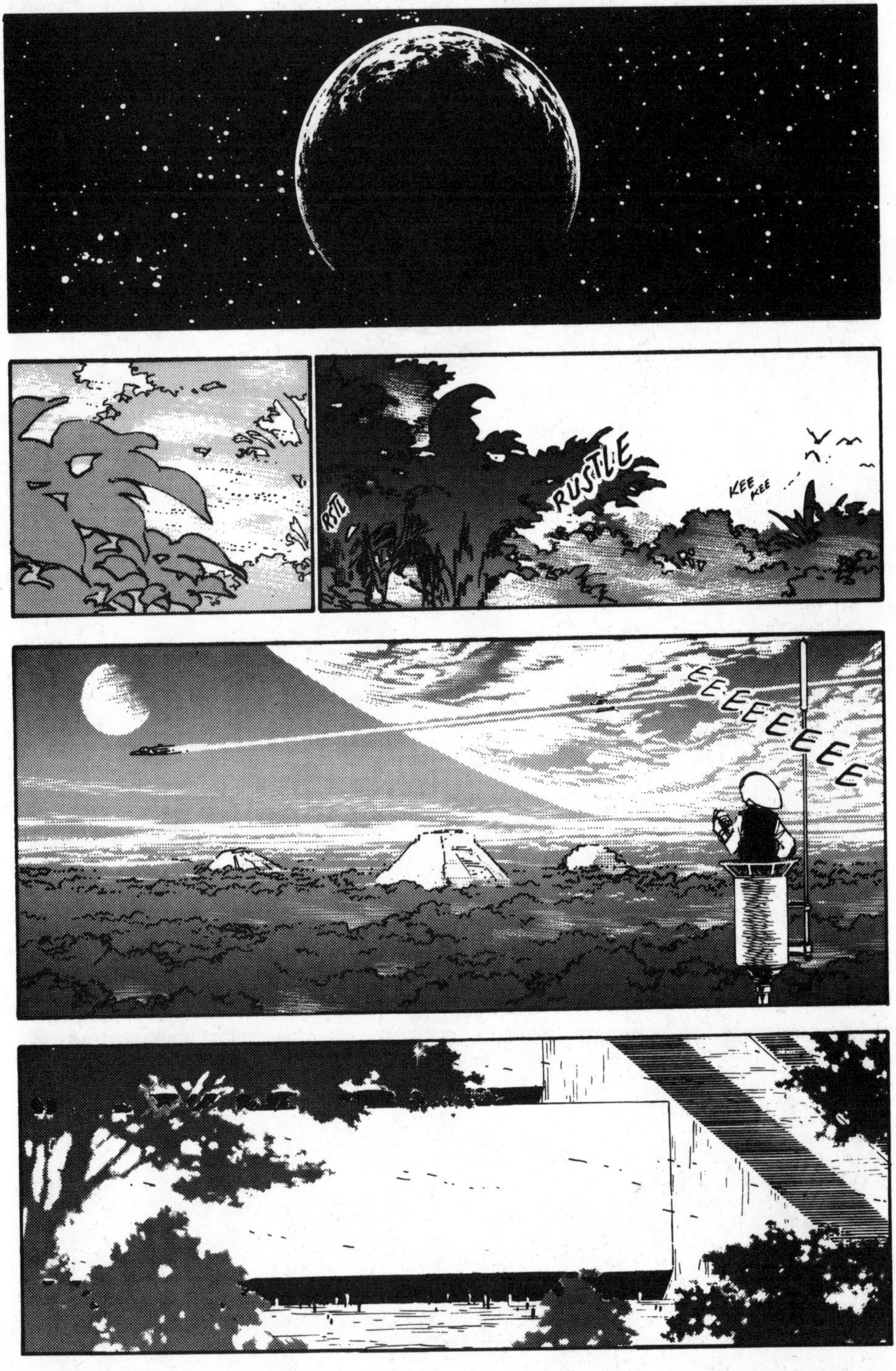
RSTL
RUSTLE
KEE KEE
EEEEEEEE

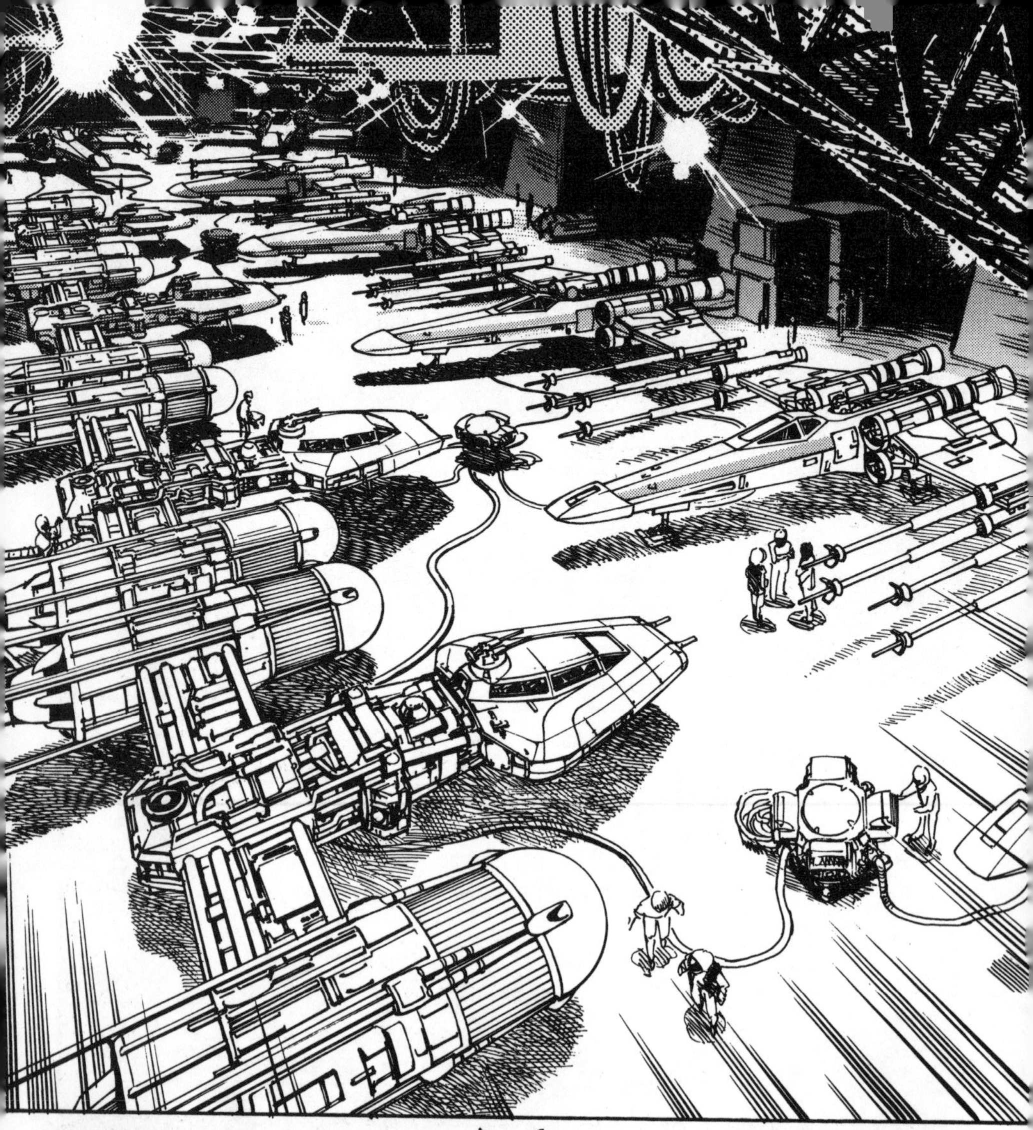

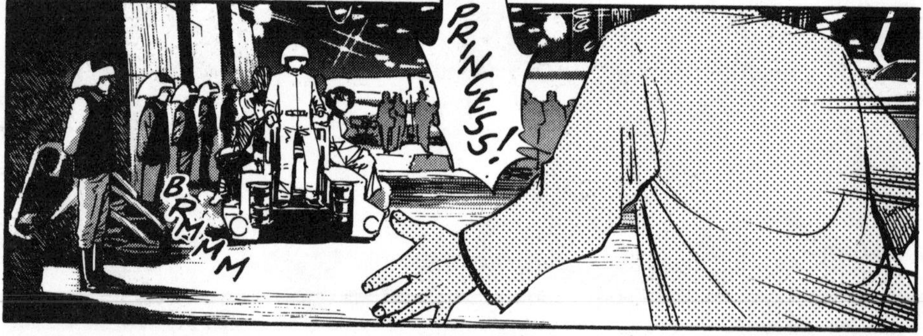
PRINCESS!
BRMMM

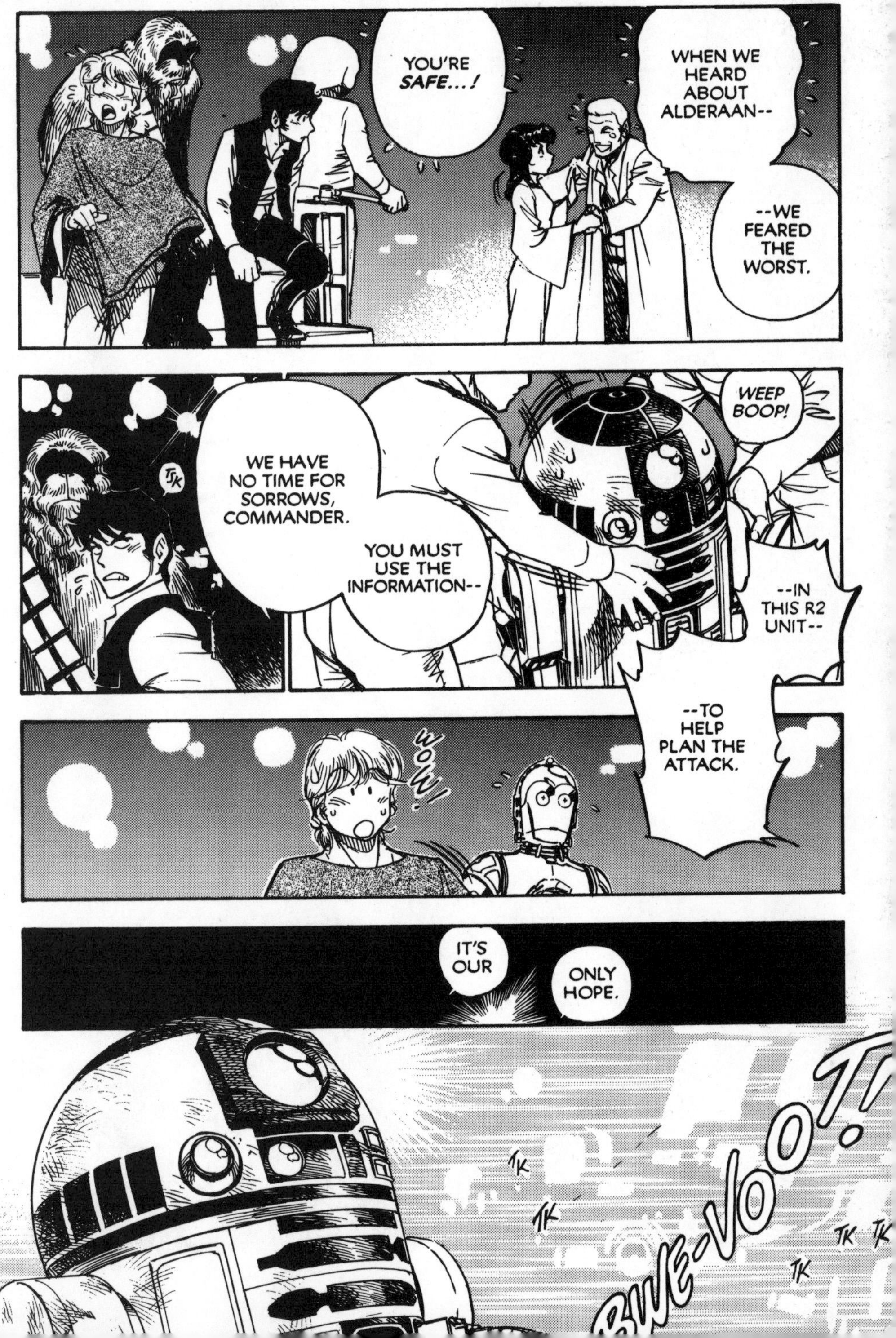
YOU'RE SAFE...!
WHEN WE HEARD ABOUT ALDERAAN--
--WE FEARED THE WORST.
TSK
WE HAVE NO TIME FOR SORROWS, COMMANDER.
YOU MUST USE THE INFORMATION--
WEEP BOOP!
--IN THIS R2 UNIT--
WOW!
--TO HELP PLAN THE ATTACK.
IT'S OUR
ONLY HOPE.
TK
TK
TK TK TK
TK
BWE-VOOT!!

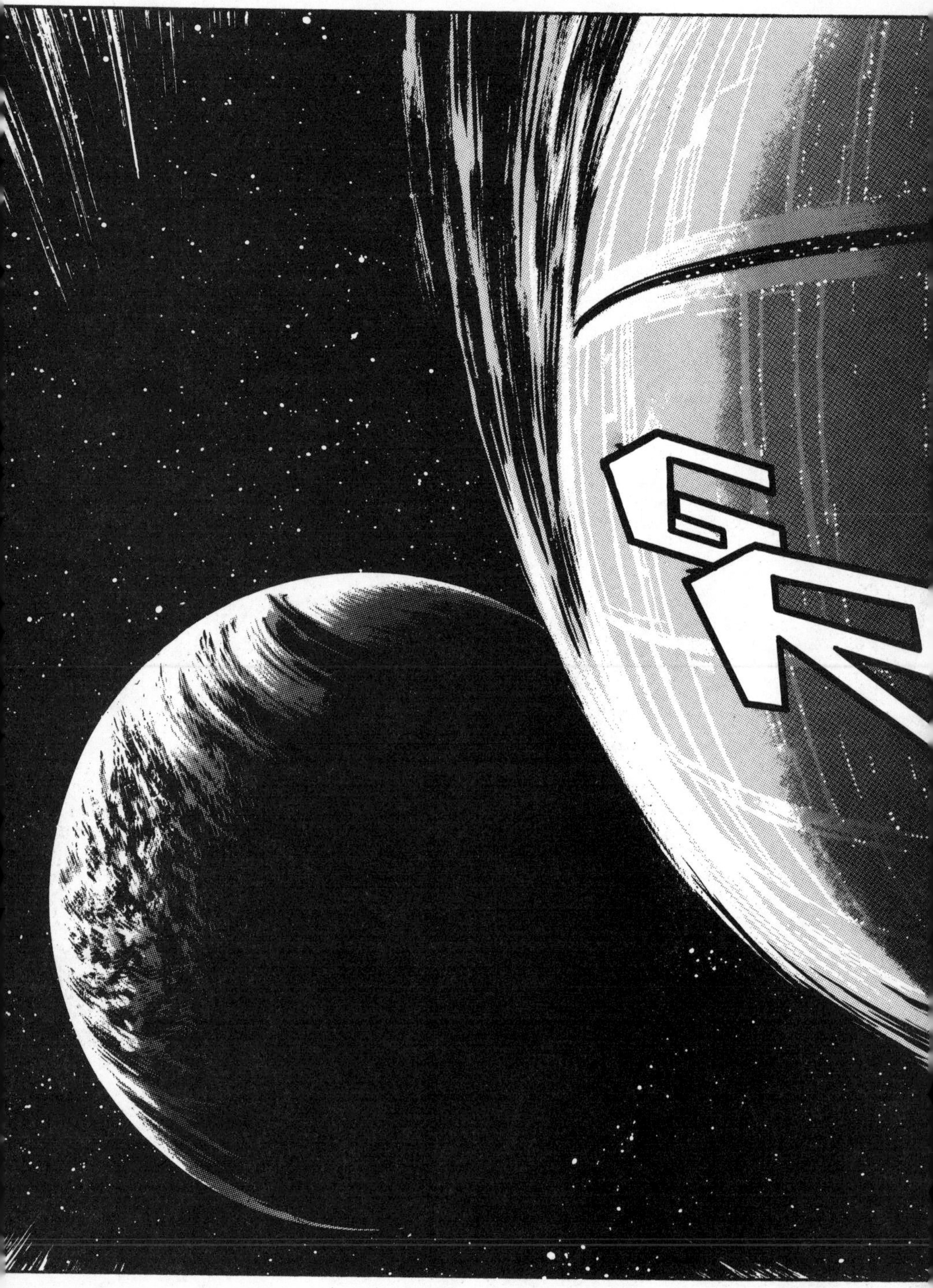
GR

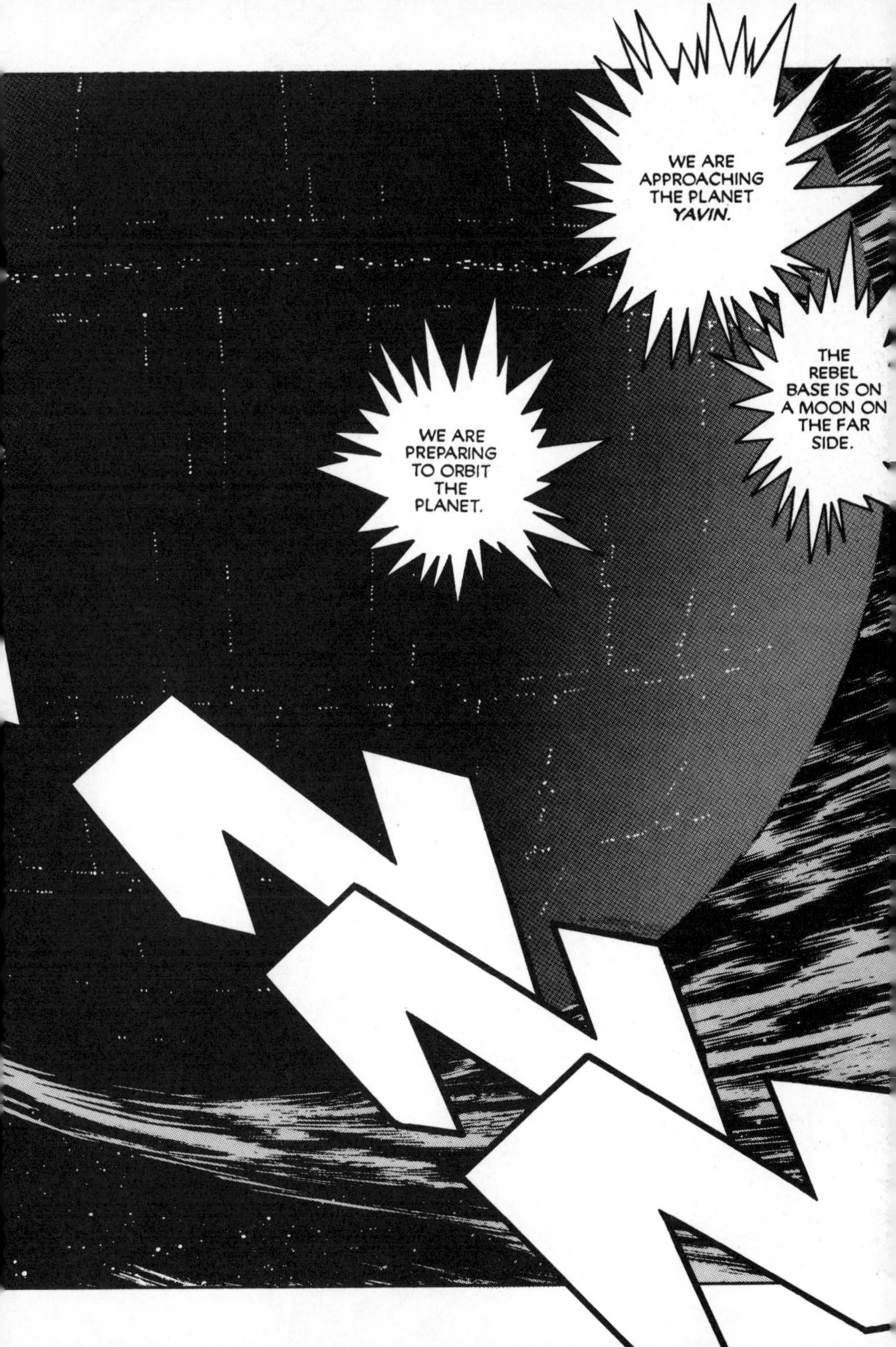
WE ARE APPROACHING THE PLANET YAVIN.
THE REBEL BASE IS ON A MOON ON THE FAR SIDE.
WE ARE PREPARING TO ORBIT THE PLANET.

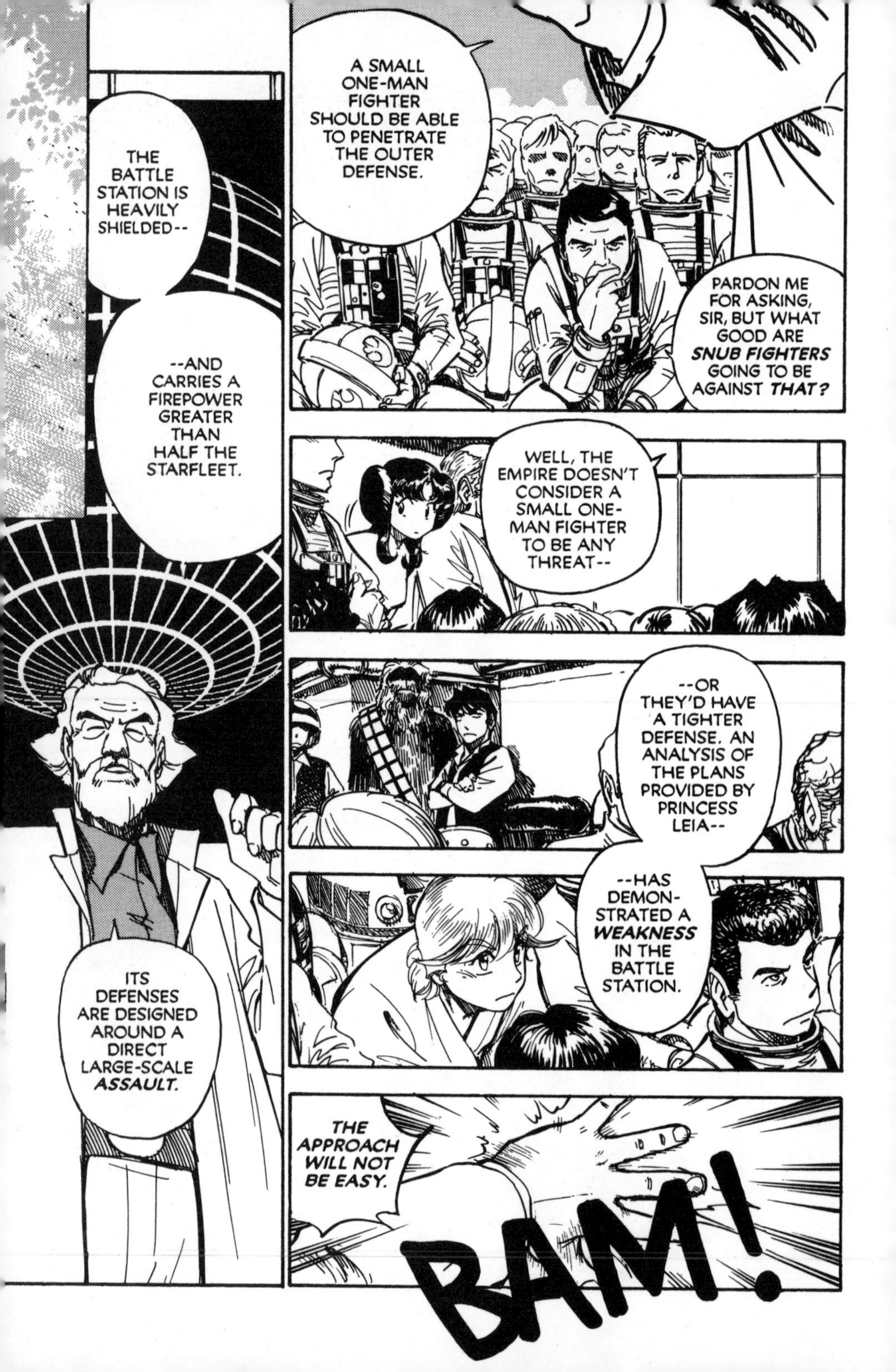
THE BATTLE STATION IS HEAVILY SHIELDED--
--AND CARRIES A FIREPOWER GREATER THAN HALF THE STARFLEET.
ITS DEFENSES ARE DESIGNED AROUND A DIRECT LARGE-SCALE ***ASSAULT.***
A SMALL ONE-MAN FIGHTER SHOULD BE ABLE TO PENETRATE THE OUTER DEFENSE.
PARDON ME FOR ASKING, SIR, BUT WHAT GOOD ARE ***SNUB FIGHTERS*** GOING TO BE AGAINST ***THAT?***
WELL, THE EMPIRE DOESN'T CONSIDER A SMALL ONE-MAN FIGHTER TO BE ANY THREAT--
--OR THEY'D HAVE A TIGHTER DEFENSE. AN ANALYSIS OF THE PLANS PROVIDED BY PRINCESS LEIA--
--HAS DEMONSTRATED A ***WEAKNESS*** IN THE BATTLE STATION.
THE APPROACH WILL NOT BE EASY.
BAM!

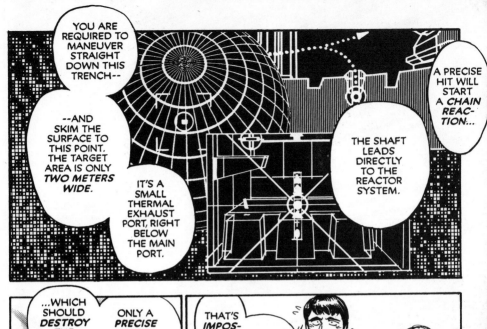

YOU ARE REQUIRED TO MANEUVER STRAIGHT DOWN THIS TRENCH--

--AND SKIM THE SURFACE TO THIS POINT. THE TARGET AREA IS ONLY *TWO METERS WIDE.*

IT'S A SMALL THERMAL EXHAUST PORT, RIGHT BELOW THE MAIN PORT.

A PRECISE HIT WILL START A *CHAIN REACTION...*

THE SHAFT LEADS DIRECTLY TO THE REACTOR SYSTEM.

...WHICH SHOULD *DESTROY* THE STATION.

ONLY A *PRECISE HIT* WILL SET UP A CHAIN REACTION.

THE SHAFT IS RAY-SHIELDED, SO YOU'LL HAVE TO USE PROTON TORPEDOES.

THAT'S IMPOSSIBLE--

--EVEN FOR A *COMPUTER.*

I USED TO BULLS-EYE *WOMP RATS* IN MY *T-SIXTEEN* BACK HOME.

THEY'RE NOT MUCH BIGGER THAN TWO METERS.

THEN...

MAN YOUR SHIPS!

AND MAY *THE FORCE* BE *WITH* YOU!

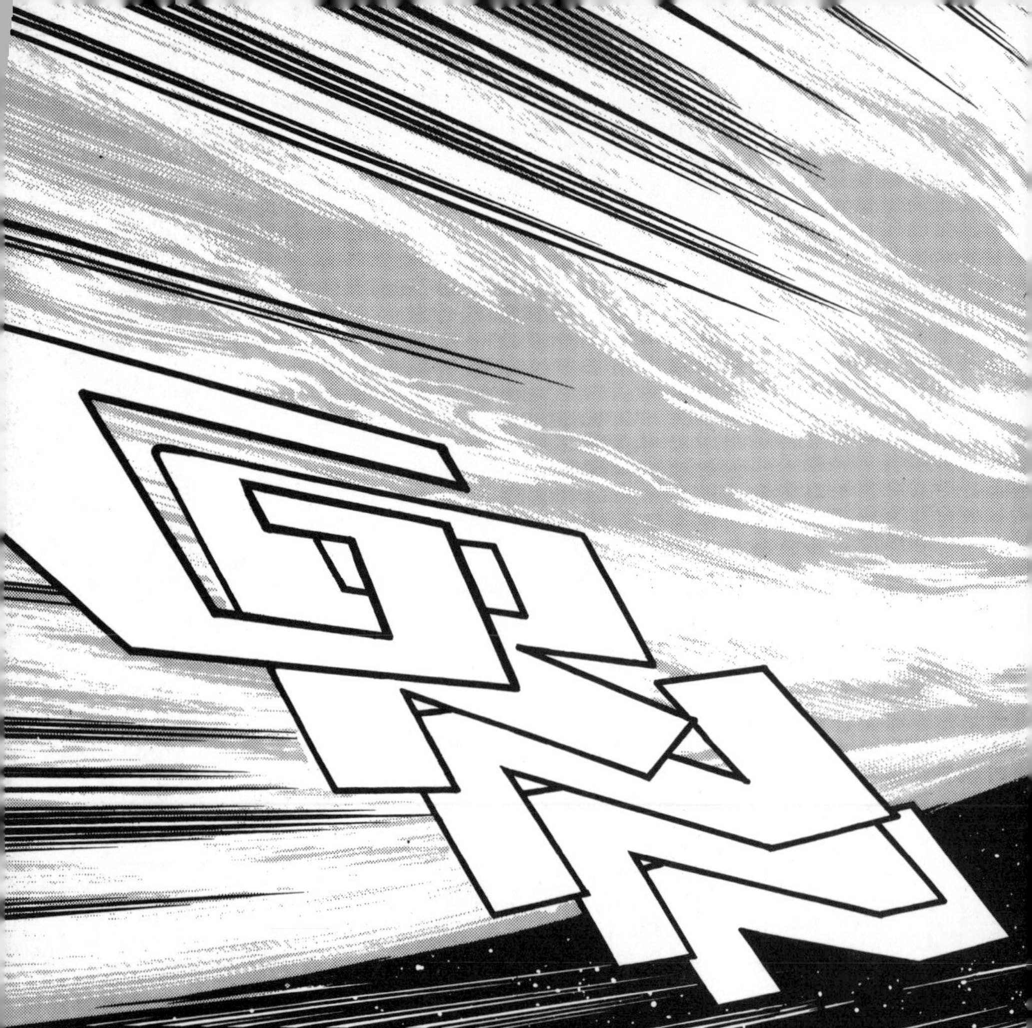

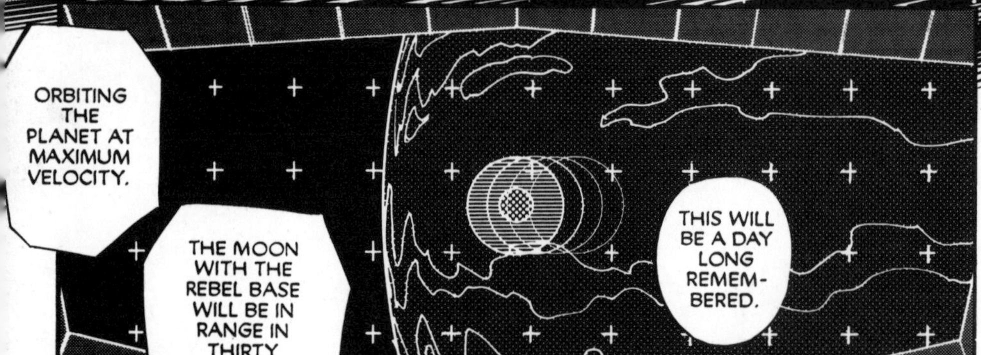
ORBITING THE PLANET AT MAXIMUM VELOCITY.
THE MOON WITH THE REBEL BASE WILL BE IN RANGE IN THIRTY MINUTES.
THIS WILL BE A DAY LONG REMEM-BERED.

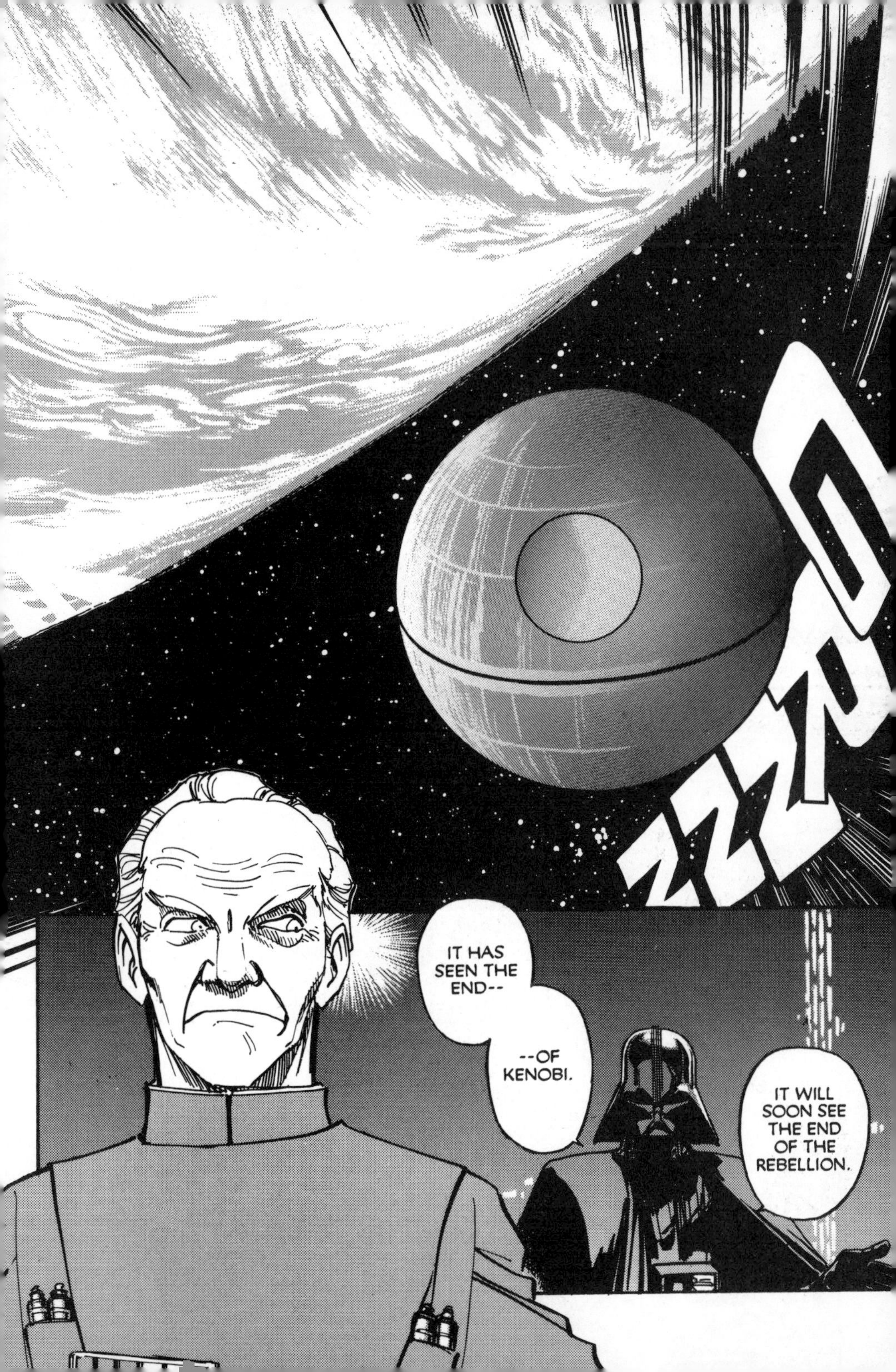
IT HAS SEEN THE END--
--OF KENOBI.
IT WILL SOON SEE THE END OF THE REBELLION.

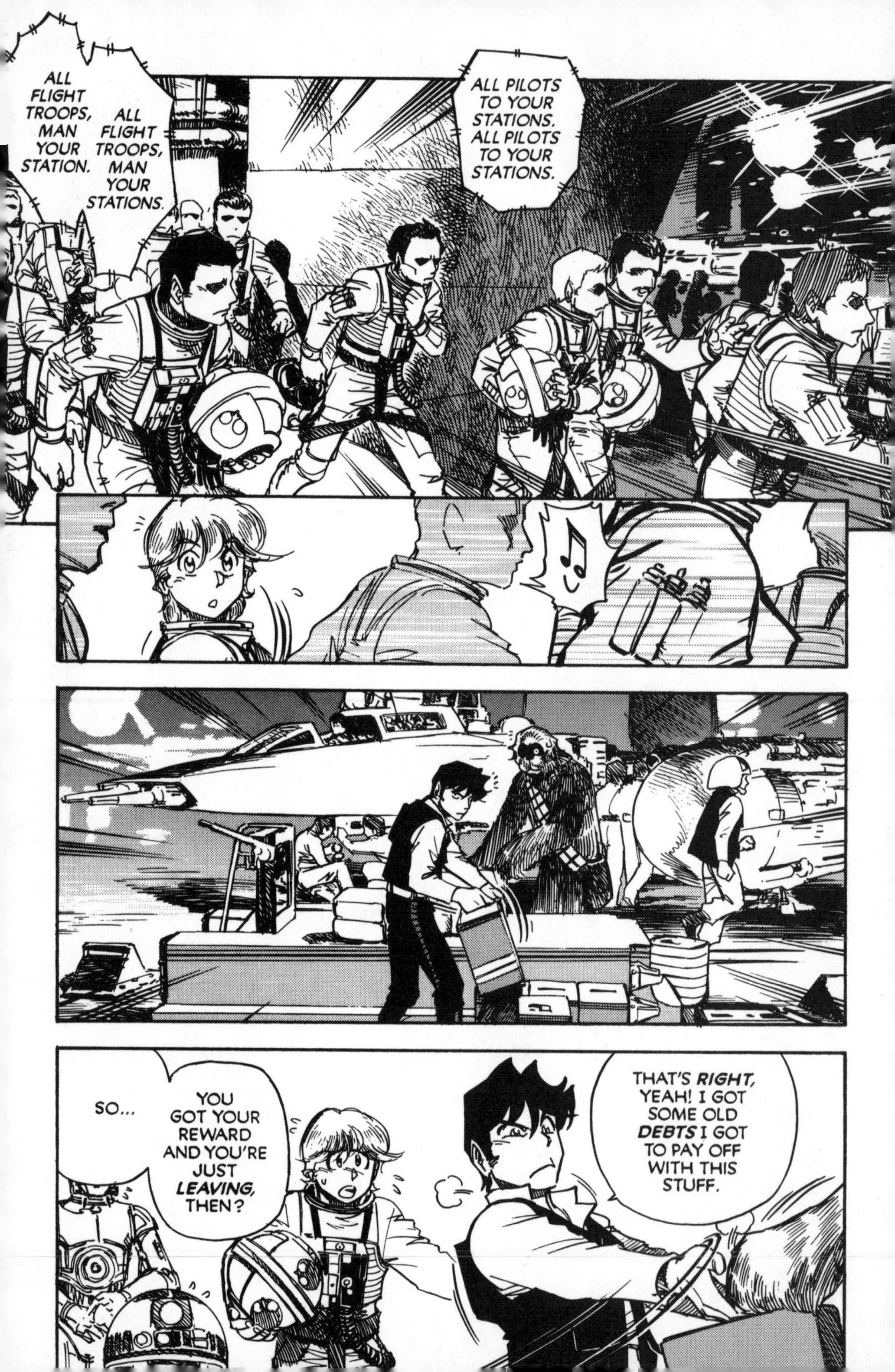
ALL FLIGHT TROOPS, MAN YOUR STATION.
ALL FLIGHT TROOPS, MAN YOUR STATIONS.
ALL PILOTS TO YOUR STATIONS. ALL PILOTS TO YOUR STATIONS.
SO...
YOU GOT YOUR REWARD AND YOU'RE JUST LEAVING, THEN?
THAT'S RIGHT, YEAH! I GOT SOME OLD DEBTS I GOT TO PAY OFF WITH THIS STUFF.

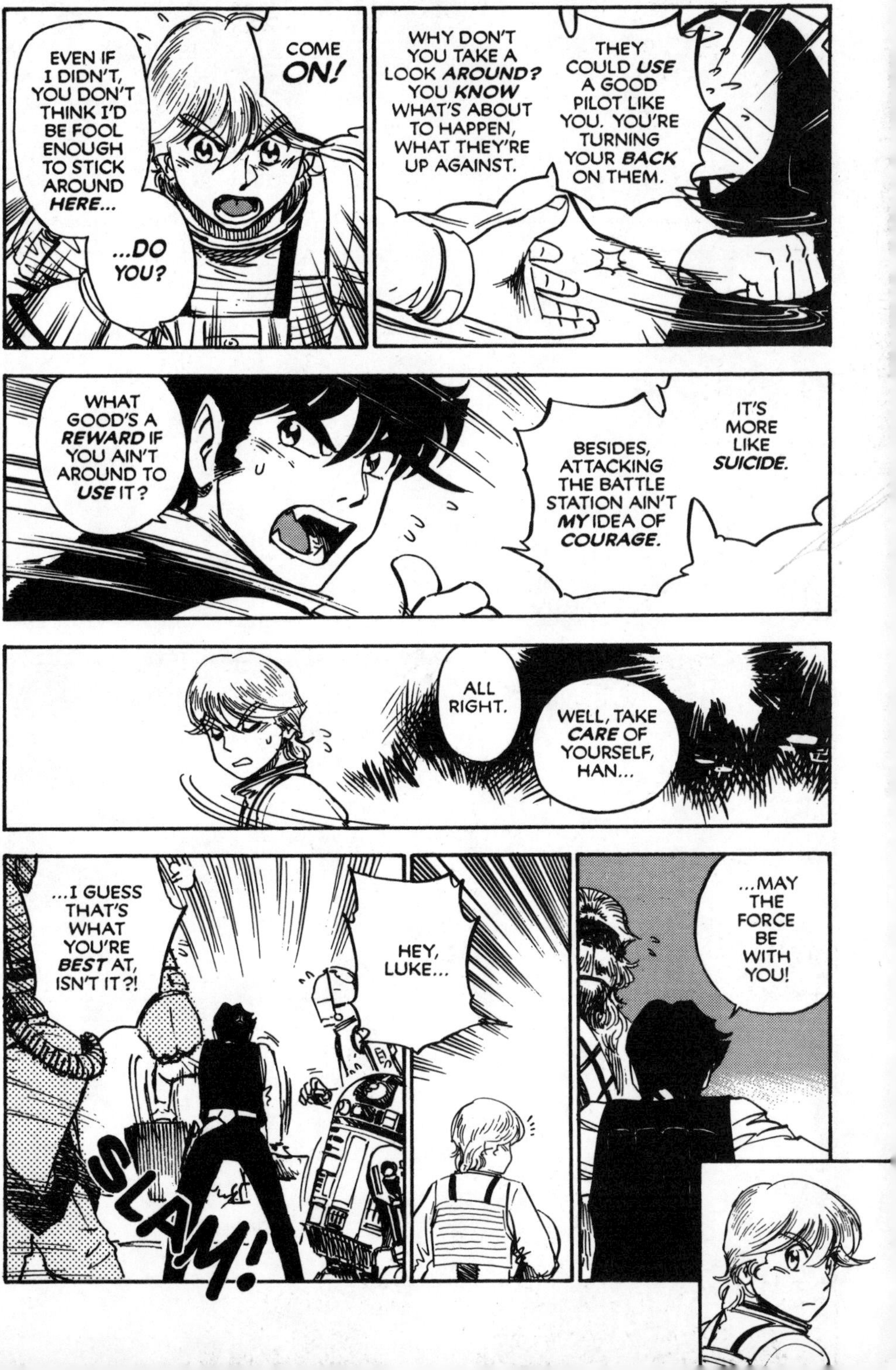
EVEN IF I DIDN'T, YOU DON'T THINK I'D BE FOOL ENOUGH TO STICK AROUND *HERE...*
COME *ON!*
...DO YOU?
WHY DON'T YOU TAKE A LOOK *AROUND?* YOU *KNOW* WHAT'S ABOUT TO HAPPEN, WHAT THEY'RE UP AGAINST.
THEY COULD *USE* A GOOD PILOT LIKE YOU. YOU'RE TURNING YOUR *BACK* ON THEM.
WHAT GOOD'S A *REWARD* IF YOU AIN'T AROUND TO *USE* IT?
BESIDES, ATTACKING THE BATTLE STATION AIN'T *MY* IDEA OF *COURAGE.*
IT'S MORE LIKE *SUICIDE.*
ALL RIGHT.
WELL, TAKE *CARE* OF YOURSELF, HAN...
...I GUESS THAT'S WHAT YOU'RE *BEST* AT, ISN'T IT?!
SLAM!
HEY, LUKE...
...MAY THE FORCE BE WITH YOU!

WHAT'S WRONG?

OH, IT'S HAN!

I DON'T KNOW, I REALLY THOUGHT HE'D CHANGE HIS MIND.

HE'S GOT TO FOLLOW HIS OWN PATH. NO ONE CAN CHOOSE IT FOR HIM.

I ONLY WISH BEN WERE HERE.

SMOOCH!

!

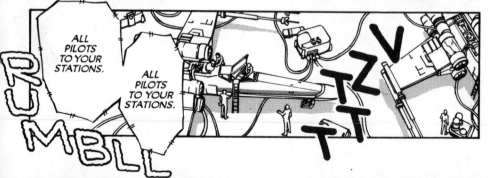

ALL PILOTS TO YOUR STATIONS.

ALL PILOTS TO YOUR STATIONS.

RUMBLL

TZV

TT

T

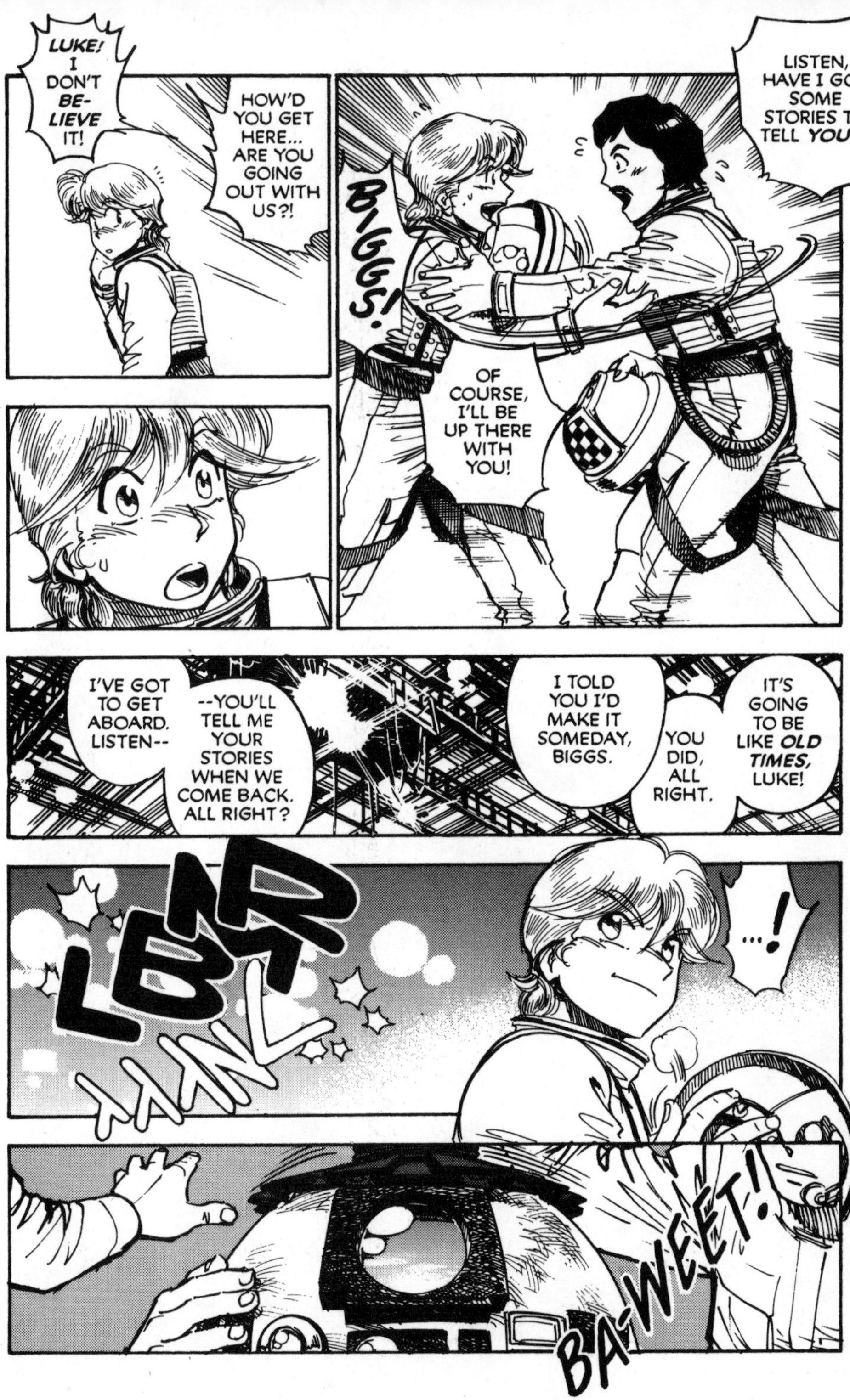

LUKE! I DON'T BE-LIEVE IT!
HOW'D YOU GET HERE... ARE YOU GOING OUT WITH US?!
LISTEN, HAVE I GOT SOME STORIES TO TELL YOU..
BIGGS!
OF COURSE, I'LL BE UP THERE WITH YOU!
I'VE GOT TO GET ABOARD. LISTEN--
--YOU'LL TELL ME YOUR STORIES WHEN WE COME BACK. ALL RIGHT?
I TOLD YOU I'D MAKE IT SOMEDAY, BIGGS.
YOU DID, ALL RIGHT.
IT'S GOING TO BE LIKE OLD TIMES, LUKE!
LBBZZT
TAANL
...!
BA-WEET!

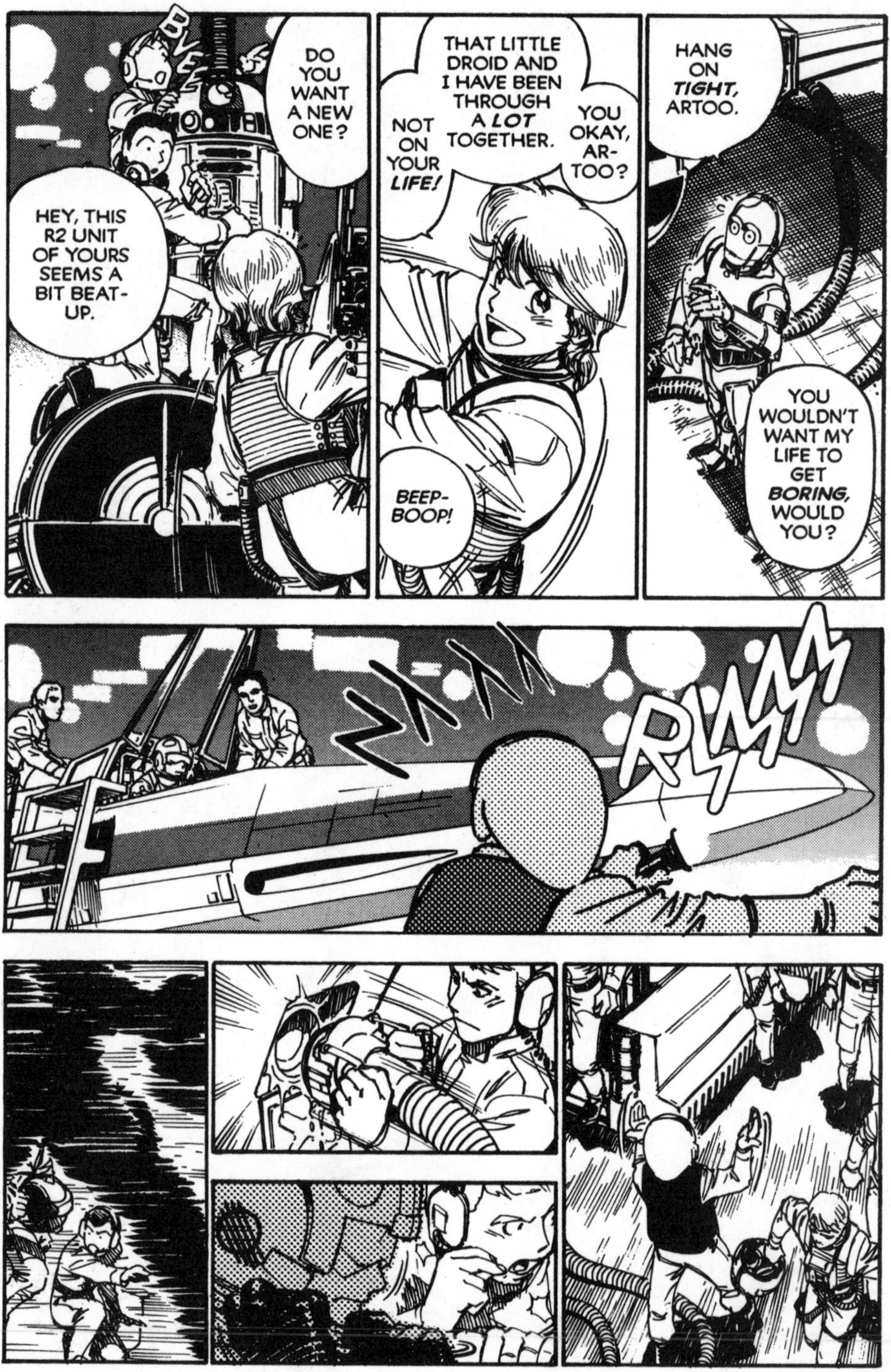
BVEE
DO YOU WANT A NEW ONE?
HEY, THIS R2 UNIT OF YOURS SEEMS A BIT BEAT-UP.
NOT ON YOUR *LIFE!*
THAT LITTLE DROID AND I HAVE BEEN THROUGH A *LOT* TOGETHER.
YOU OKAY, AR-TOO?
BEEP-BOOP!
HANG ON *TIGHT,* ARTOO.
YOU WOULDN'T WANT MY LIFE TO GET *BORING,* WOULD YOU?

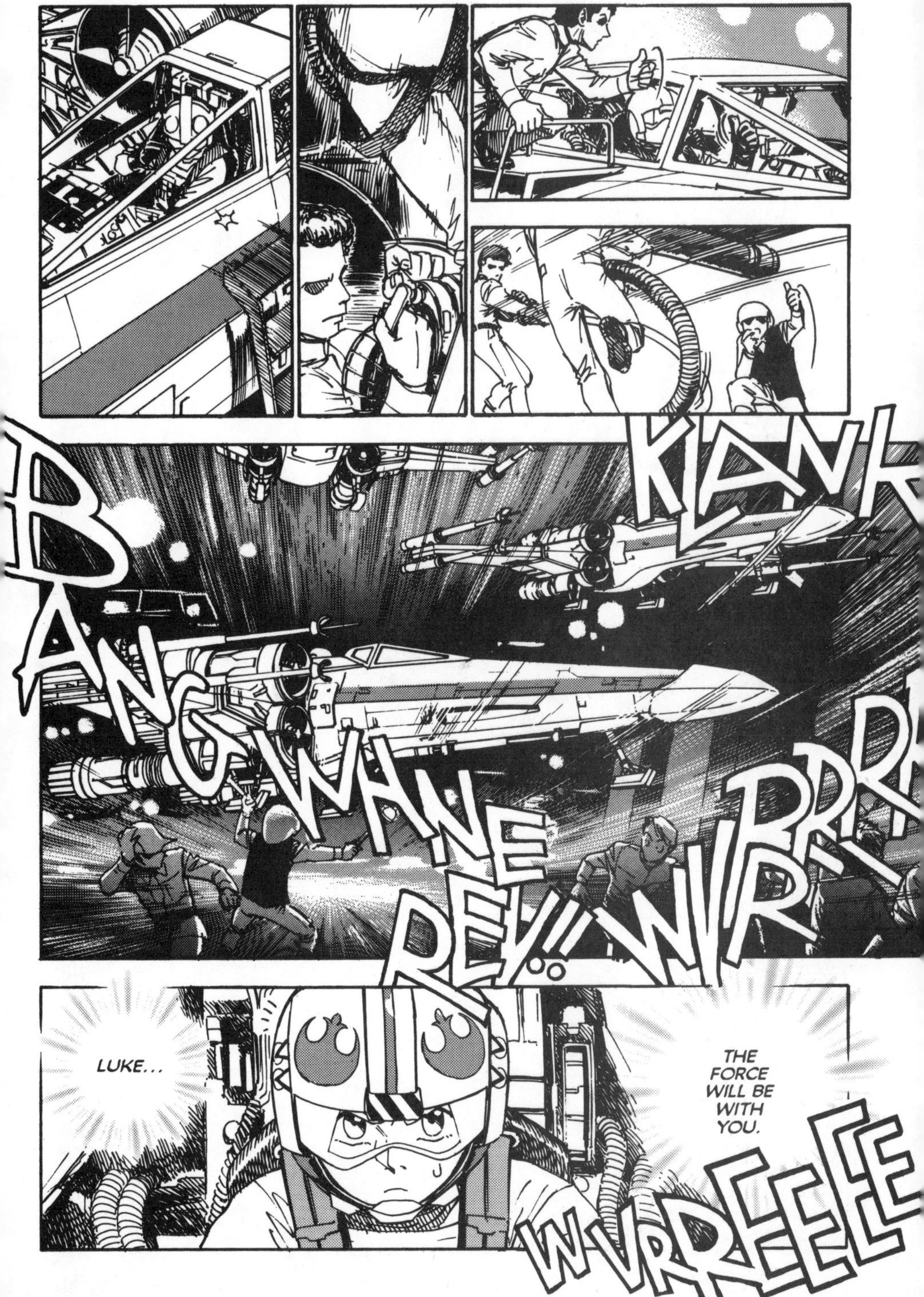

BANG
KLANK
WHINE
REV!!
WIRR
LUKE...
THE FORCE WILL BE WITH YOU.
WVREEEEE

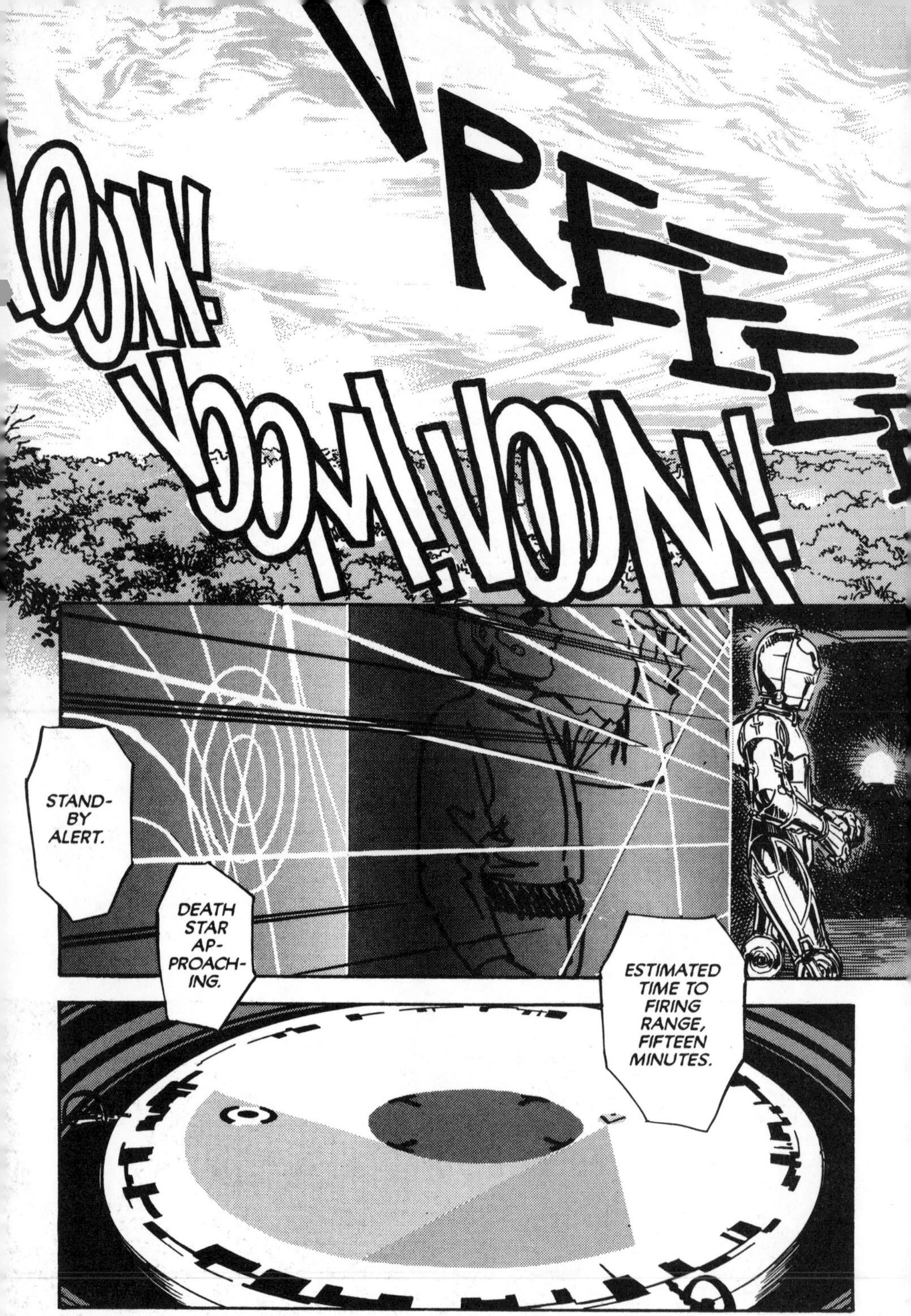
OOM!
VREEEEE
VOOM! VOOM!
STAND-BY ALERT.
DEATH STAR AP-PROACH-ING.
ESTIMATED TIME TO FIRING RANGE, FIFTEEN MINUTES.

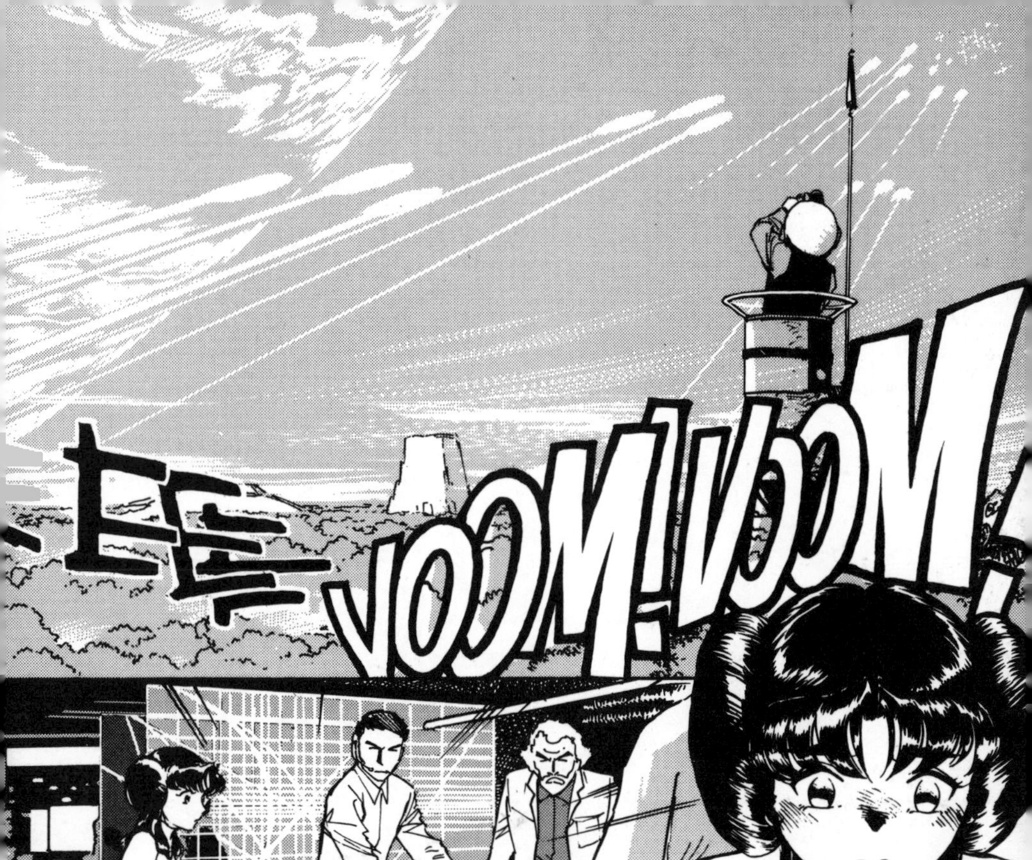
VOOM! VOOM!

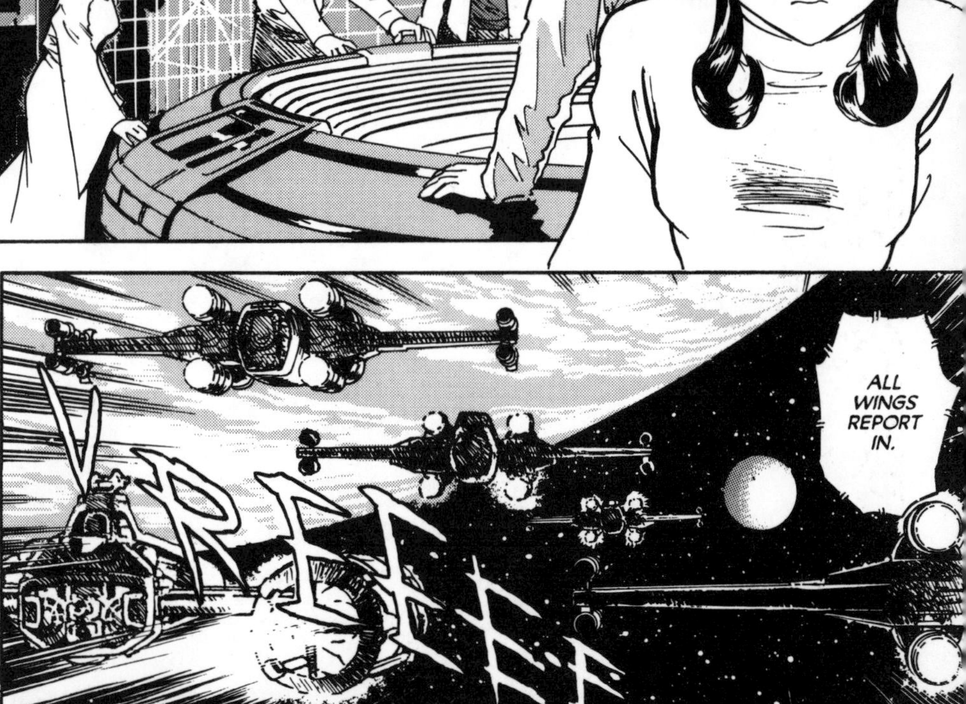
VREEE
ALL WINGS REPORT IN.

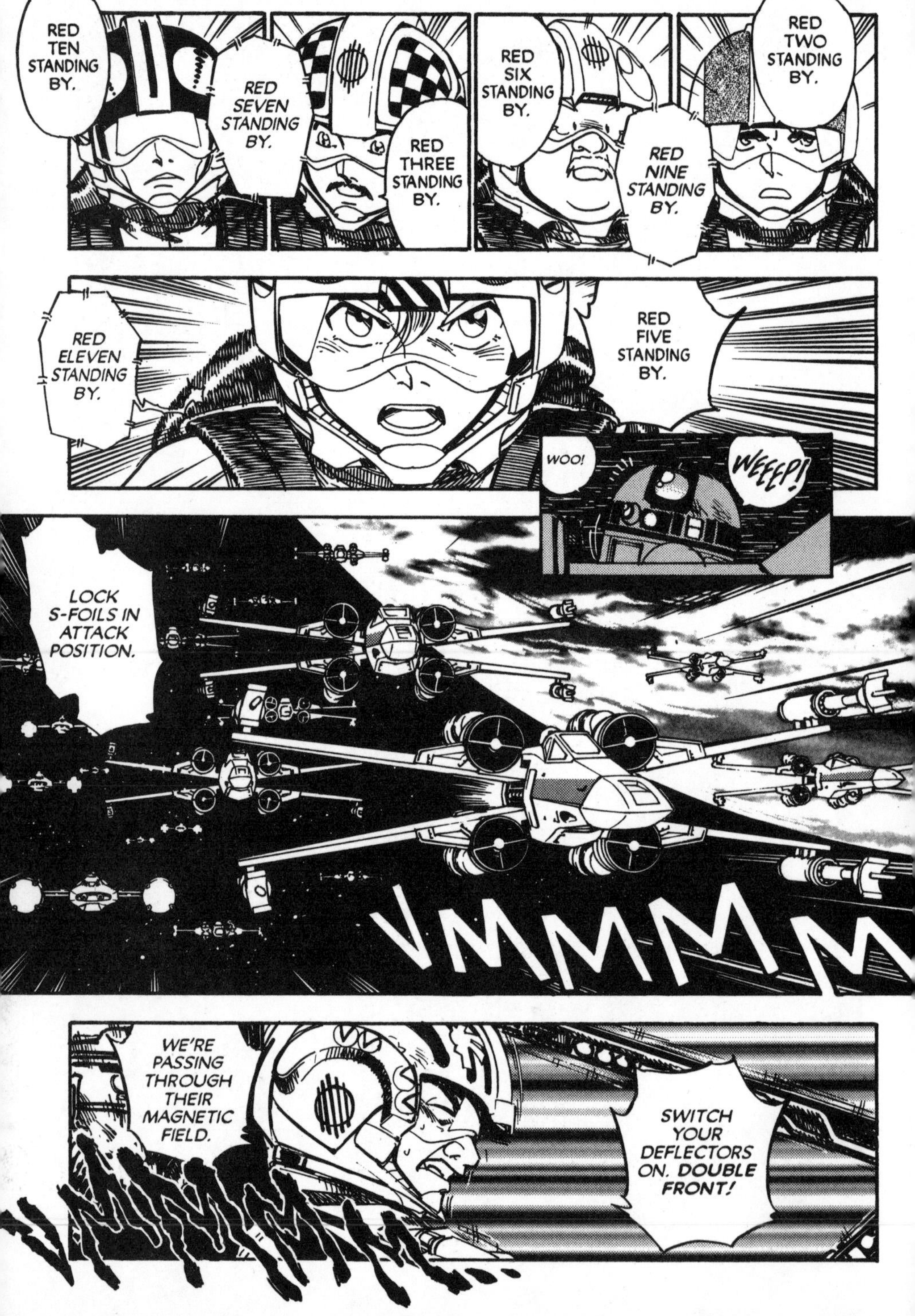
RED TEN STANDING BY.
RED SEVEN STANDING BY.
RED THREE STANDING BY.
RED SIX STANDING BY.
RED NINE STANDING BY.
RED TWO STANDING BY.
RED ELEVEN STANDING BY.
RED FIVE STANDING BY.
WOO!
WEEEP!
LOCK S-FOILS IN ATTACK POSITION.
VMMMM
WE'RE PASSING THROUGH THEIR MAGNETIC FIELD.
SWITCH YOUR DEFLECTORS ON. DOUBLE FRONT!

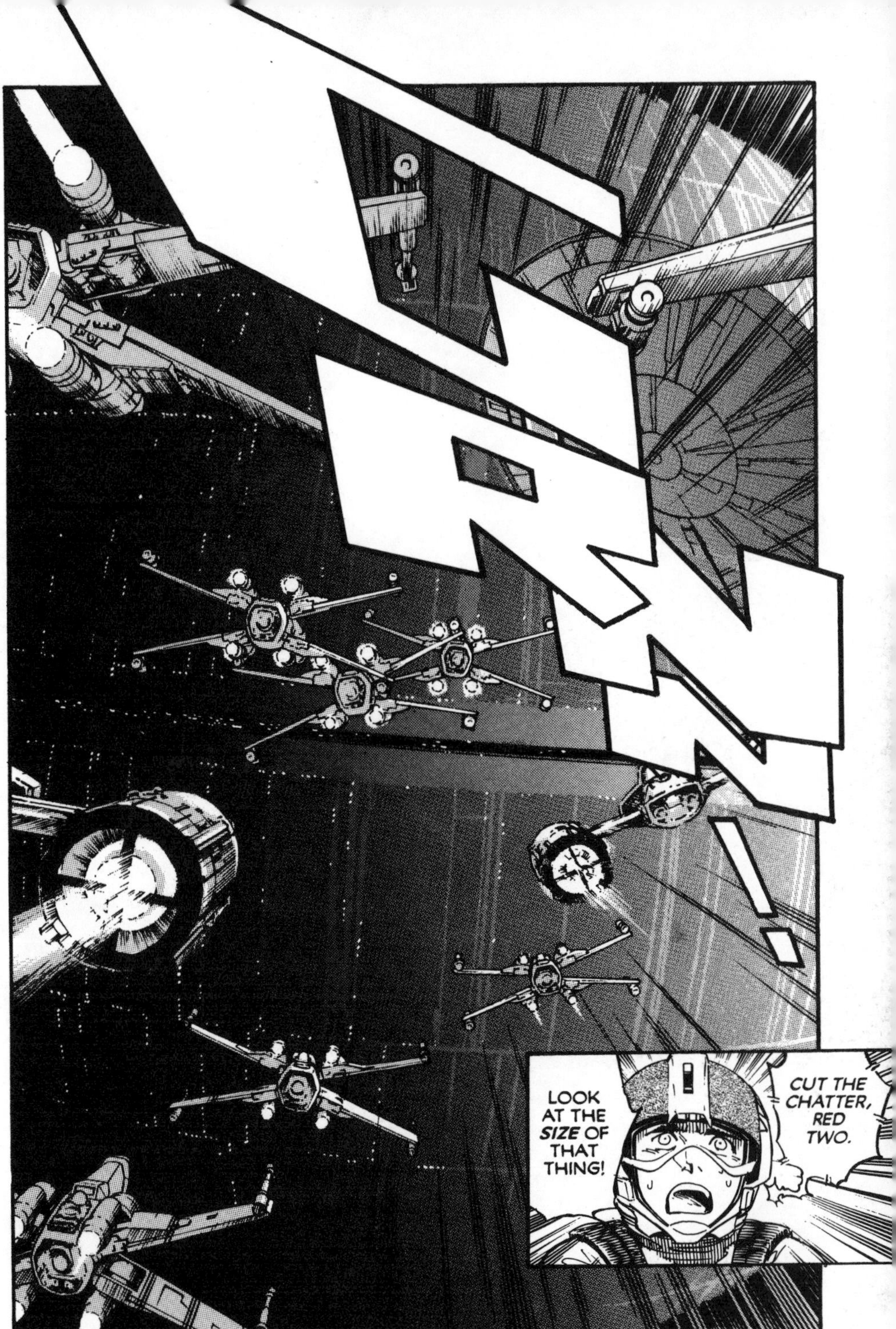
LOOK AT THE *SIZE* OF THAT THING!
CUT THE CHATTER, RED TWO.

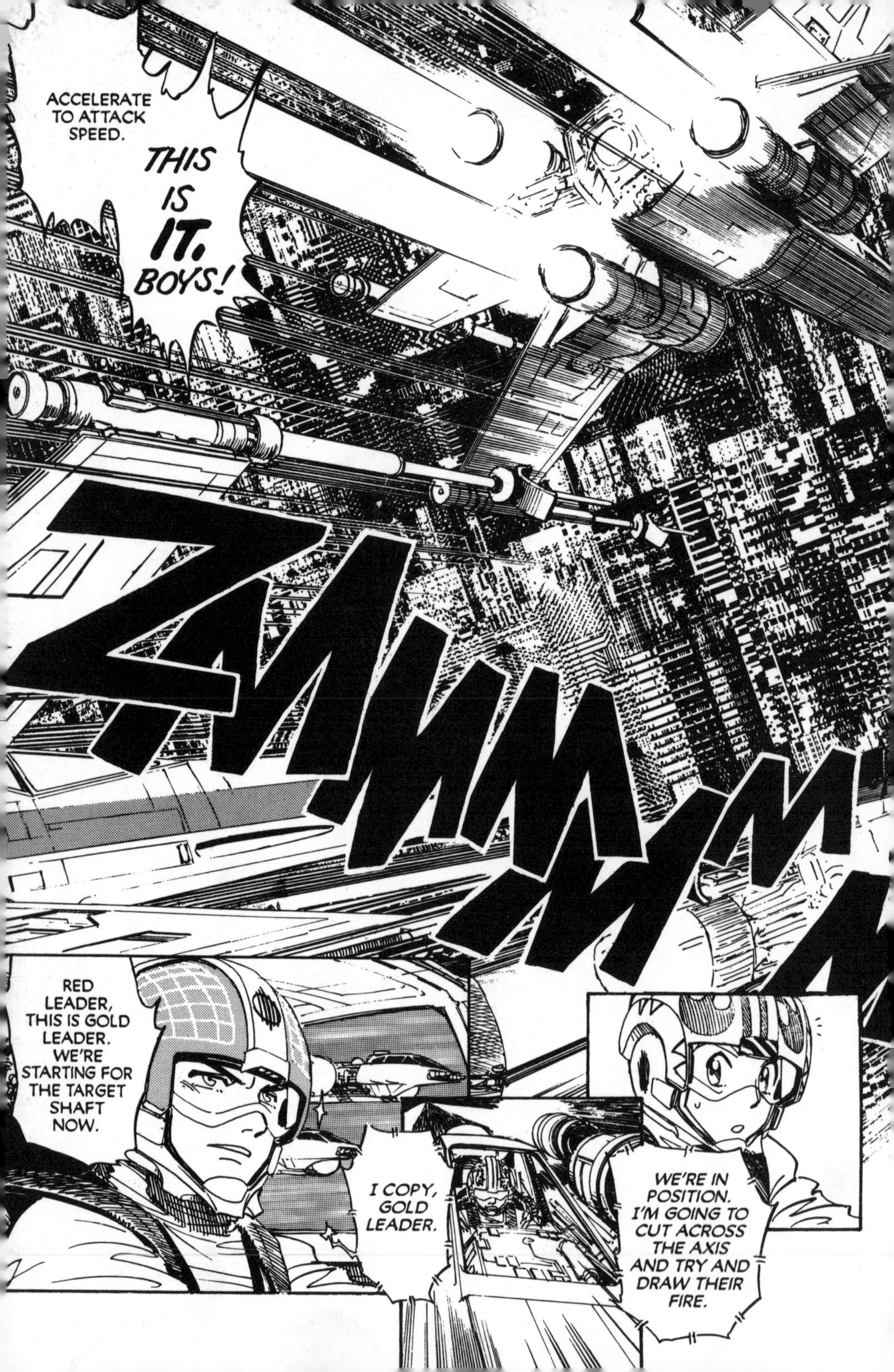
ACCELERATE TO ATTACK SPEED.
THIS IS IT, BOYS!
ZMMMMM
RED LEADER, THIS IS GOLD LEADER. WE'RE STARTING FOR THE TARGET SHAFT NOW.
I COPY, GOLD LEADER.
WE'RE IN POSITION. I'M GOING TO CUT ACROSS THE AXIS AND TRY AND DRAW THEIR FIRE.

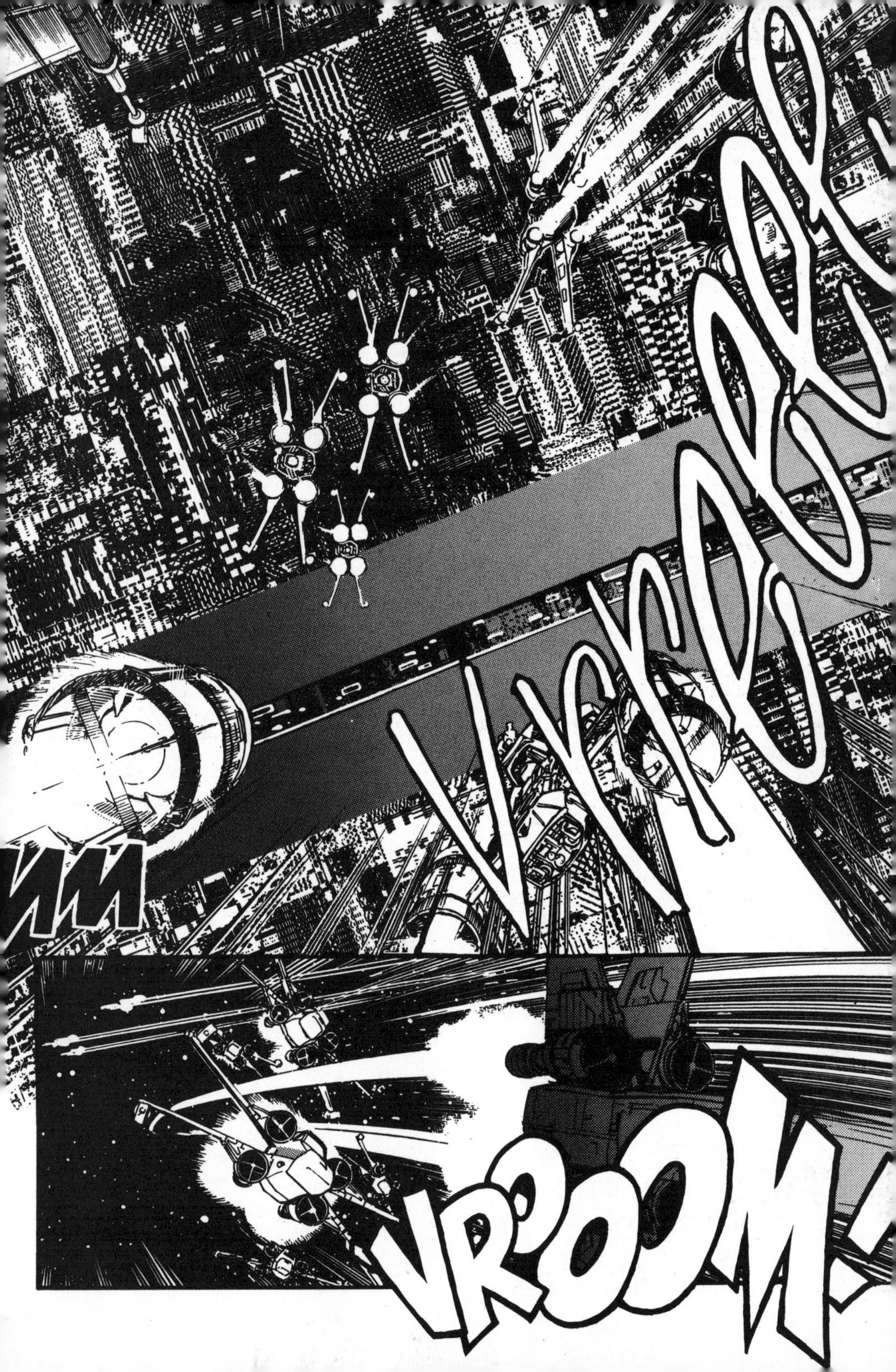
VROOM

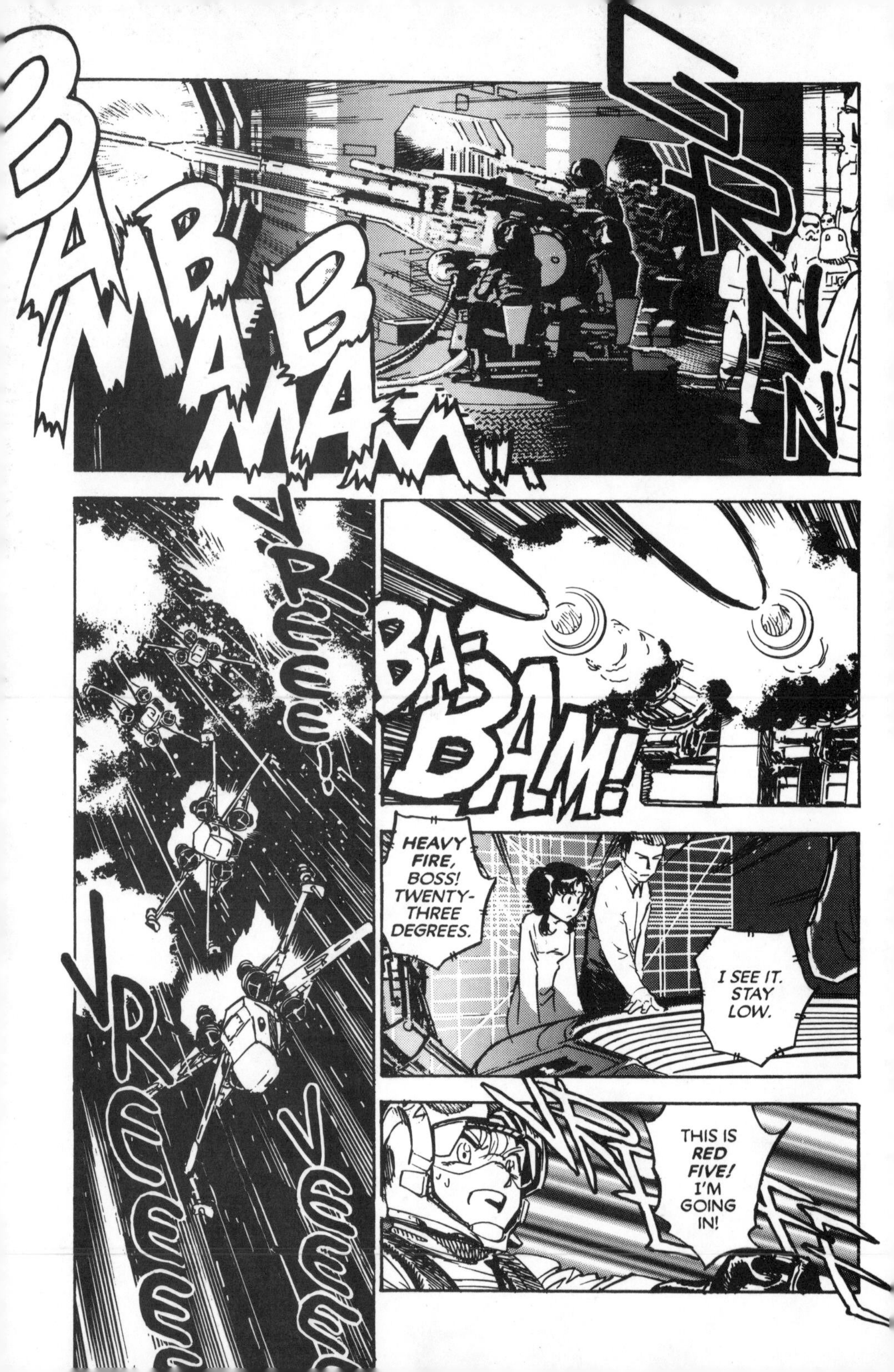
VREEE!
BA-BAM!
HEAVY FIRE, BOSS! TWENTY-THREE DEGREES.
I SEE IT. STAY LOW.
THIS IS RED FIVE! I'M GOING IN!

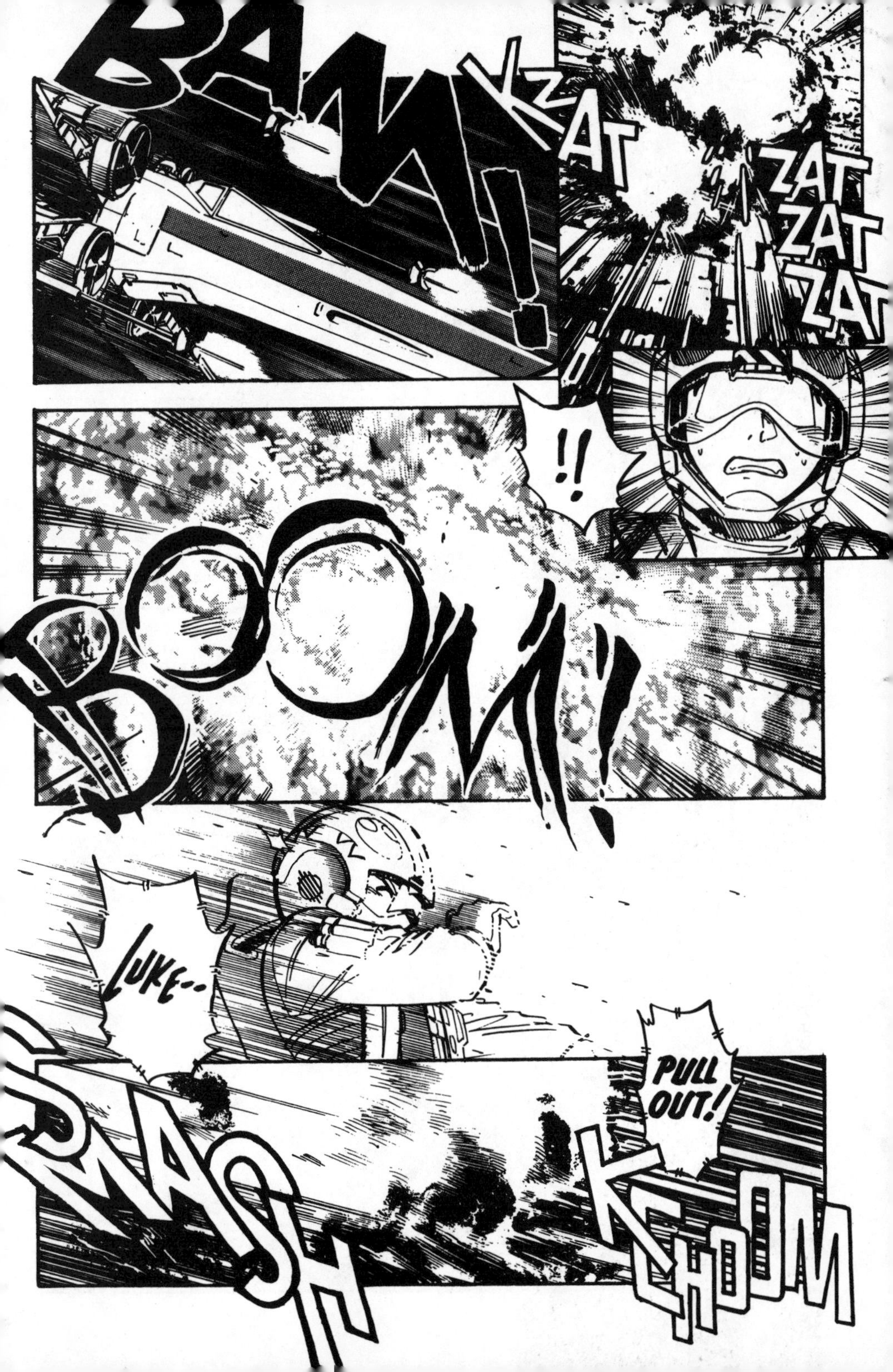
BAMM!
ZZAT
ZAT
ZAT
ZAT
!!
BOOM!
LUKE--
PULL OUT!
SMASH
KCHOOM

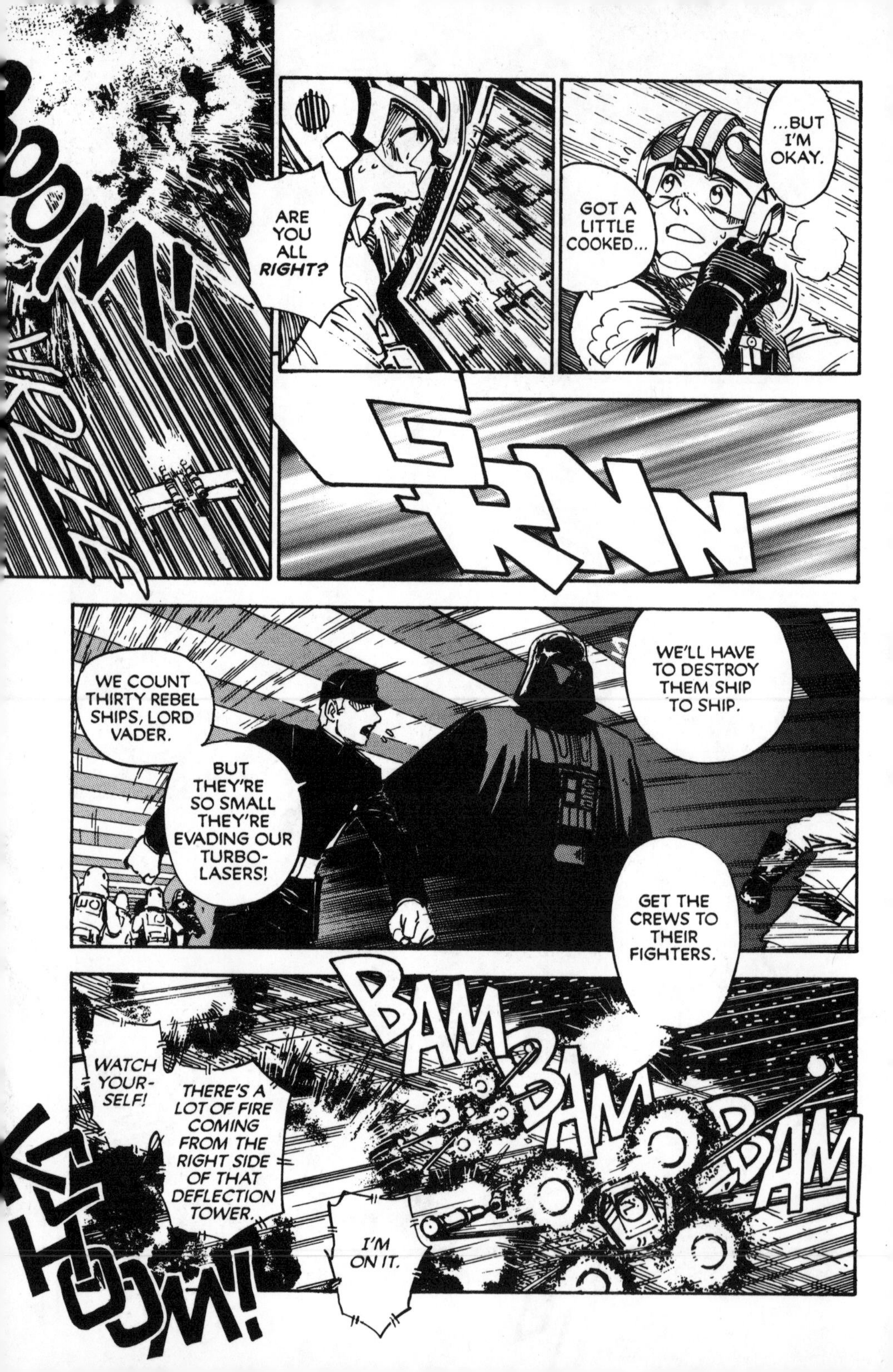

BOOM!
ARE YOU ALL RIGHT?
GOT A LITTLE COOKED...
...BUT I'M OKAY.
GRNN
WE COUNT THIRTY REBEL SHIPS, LORD VADER.
BUT THEY'RE SO SMALL THEY'RE EVADING OUR TURBO-LASERS!
WE'LL HAVE TO DESTROY THEM SHIP TO SHIP.
GET THE CREWS TO THEIR FIGHTERS.
KA-THOOM!
WATCH YOUR-SELF!
THERE'S A LOT OF FIRE COMING FROM THE RIGHT SIDE OF THAT DEFLECTION TOWER.
I'M ON IT.
BAM BAM BAM BAM

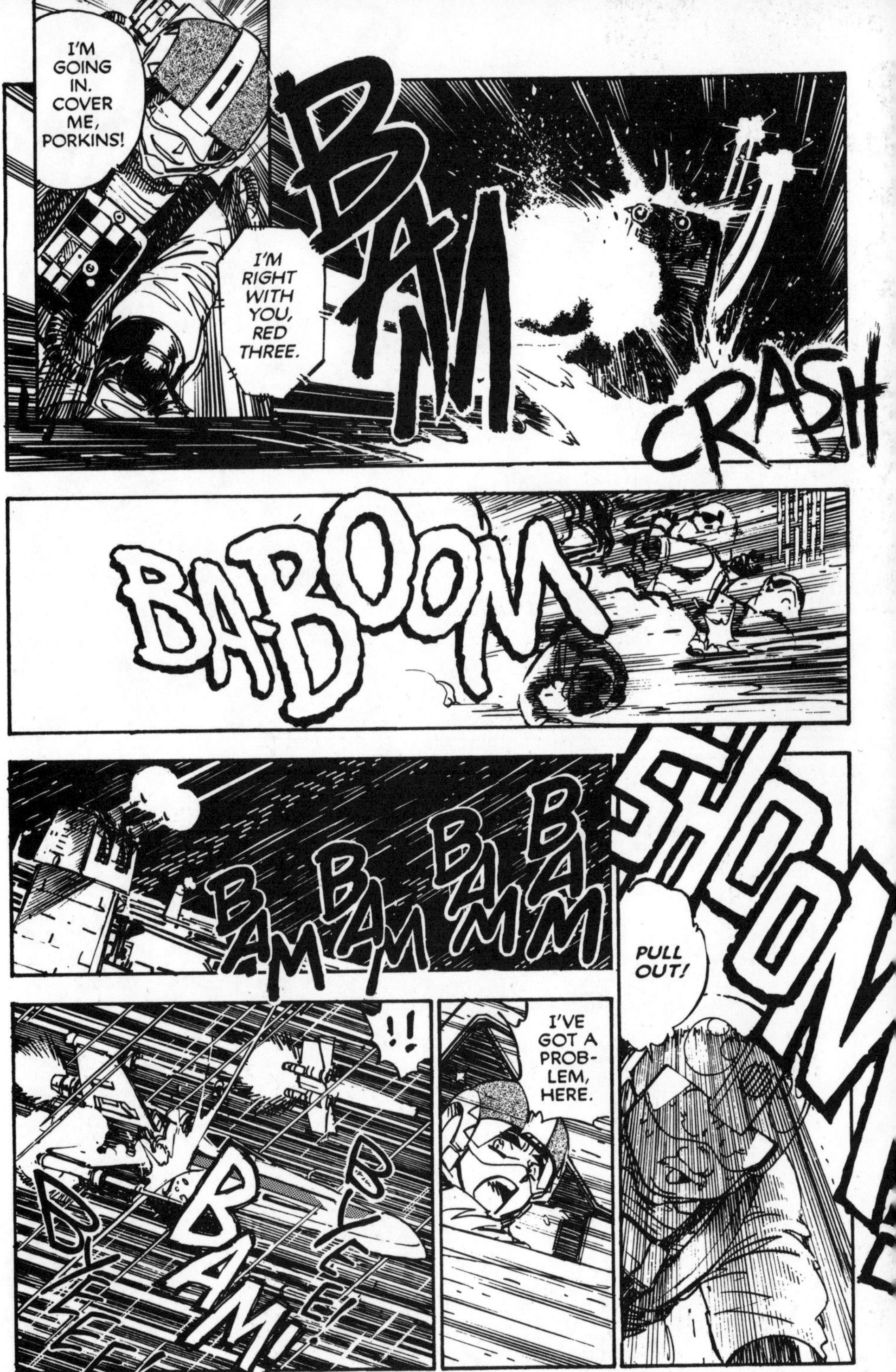
I'M GOING IN. COVER ME, PORKINS!
I'M RIGHT WITH YOU, RED THREE.
BAM
CRASH
BA-BOOM
BAM BAM BAAM BAAMM
!!
BAM!
I'VE GOT A PROB-LEM, HERE.
PULL OUT!
SHOOM

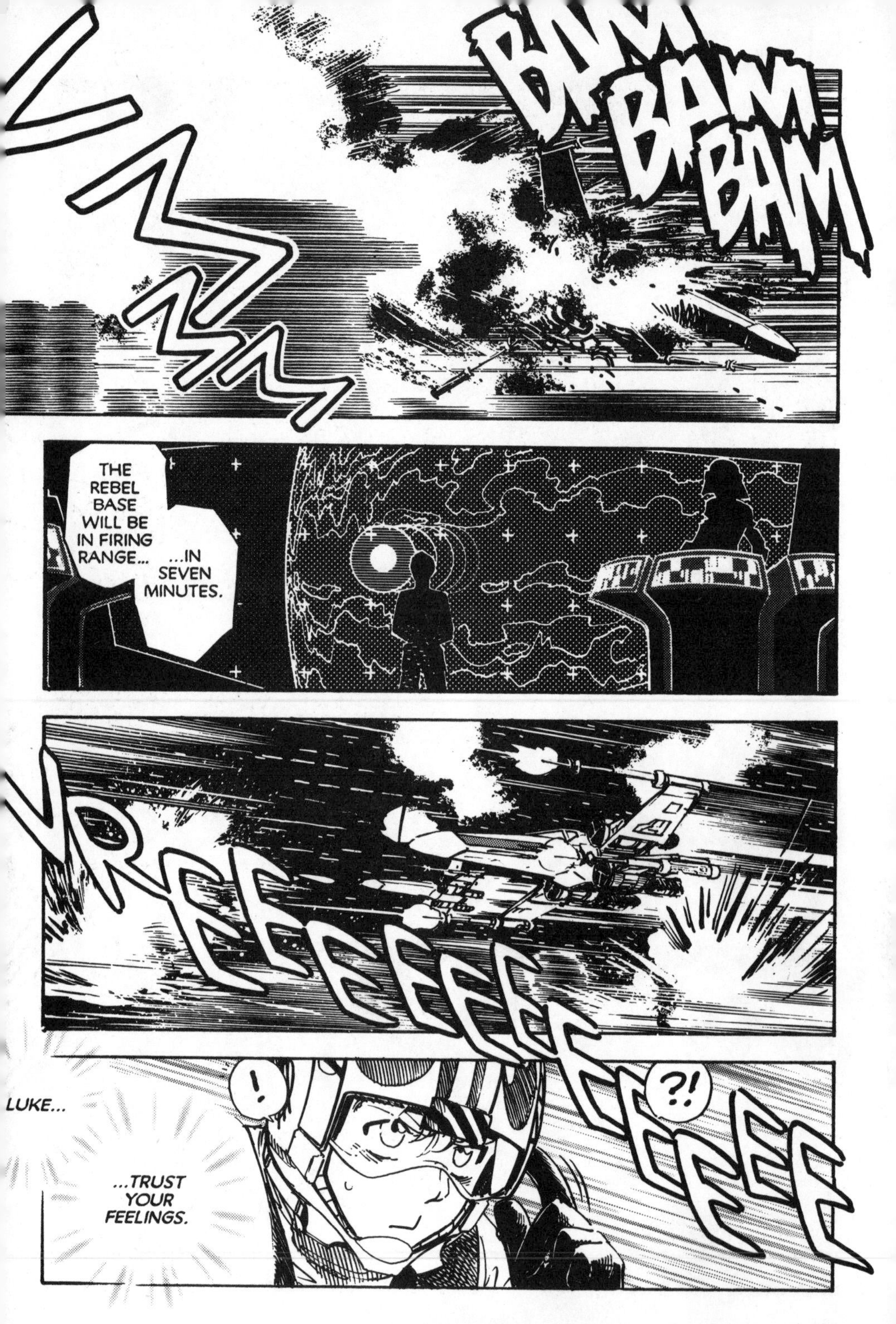

BAM
BAM
BAM
THE REBEL BASE WILL BE IN FIRING RANGE...
...IN SEVEN MINUTES.
VREEEEEEEEEEEEEE
!
?!
LUKE...
...TRUST YOUR FEELINGS.

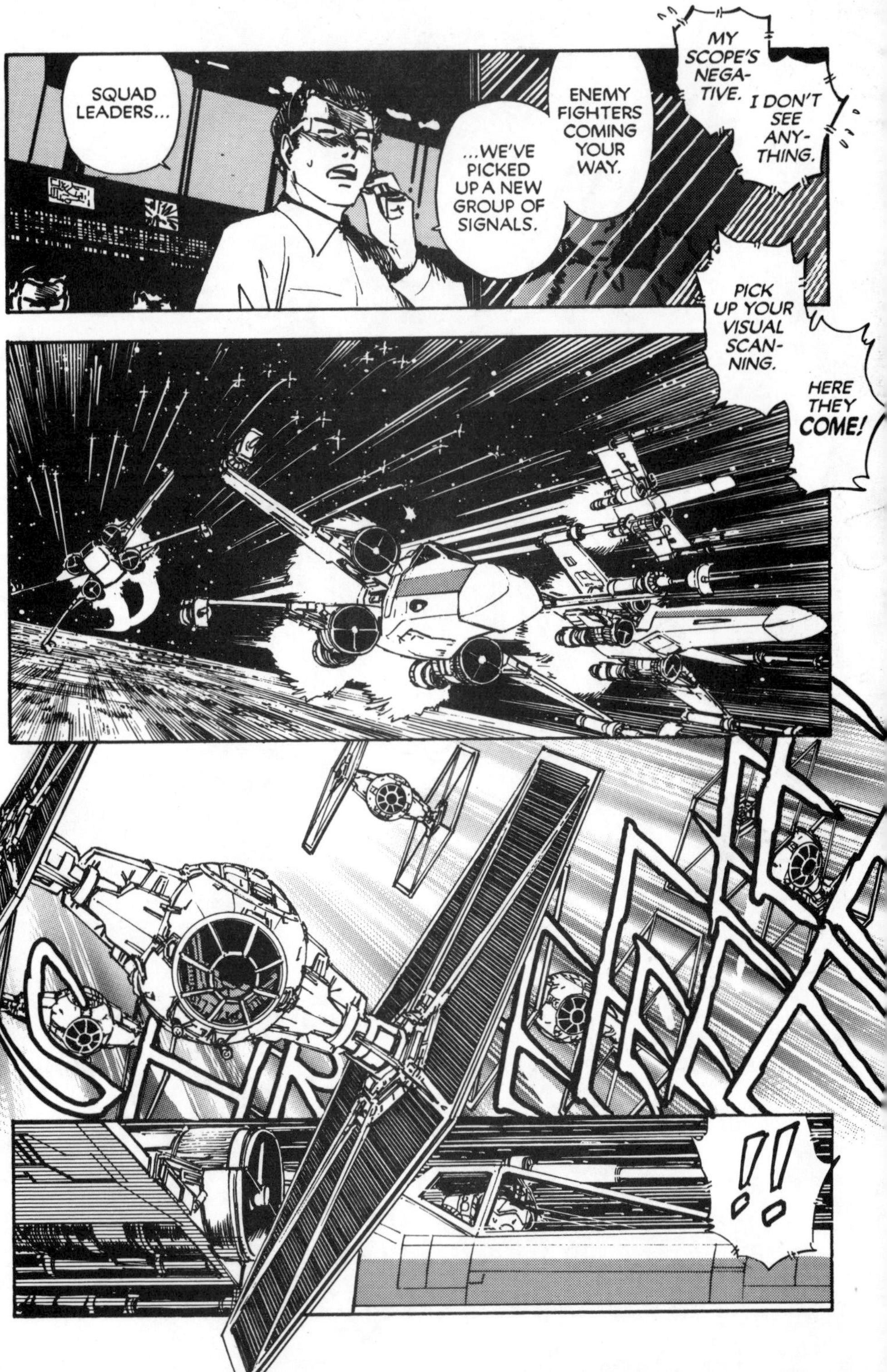
SQUAD LEADERS...
...WE'VE PICKED UP A NEW GROUP OF SIGNALS.
ENEMY FIGHTERS COMING YOUR WAY.
MY SCOPE'S NEGA-TIVE.
I DON'T SEE ANY-THING.
PICK UP YOUR VISUAL SCAN-NING.
HERE THEY COME!
!!

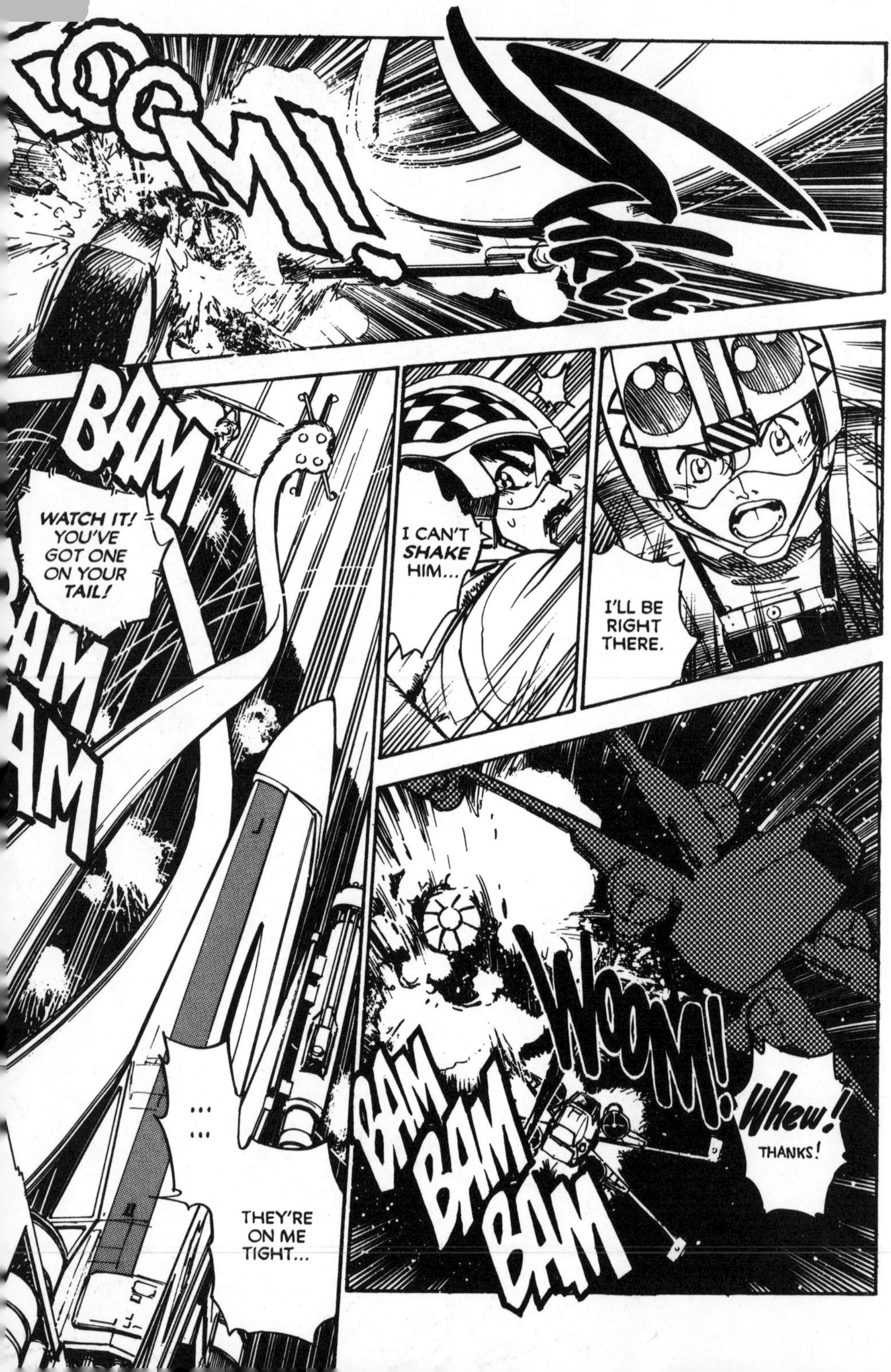

BAM
WATCH IT! YOU'VE GOT ONE ON YOUR TAIL!
BAM BAM
...
...
THEY'RE ON ME TIGHT...
I CAN'T SHAKE HIM...
I'LL BE RIGHT THERE.
WOOM!
BAM BAM BAM
Whew!
THANKS!

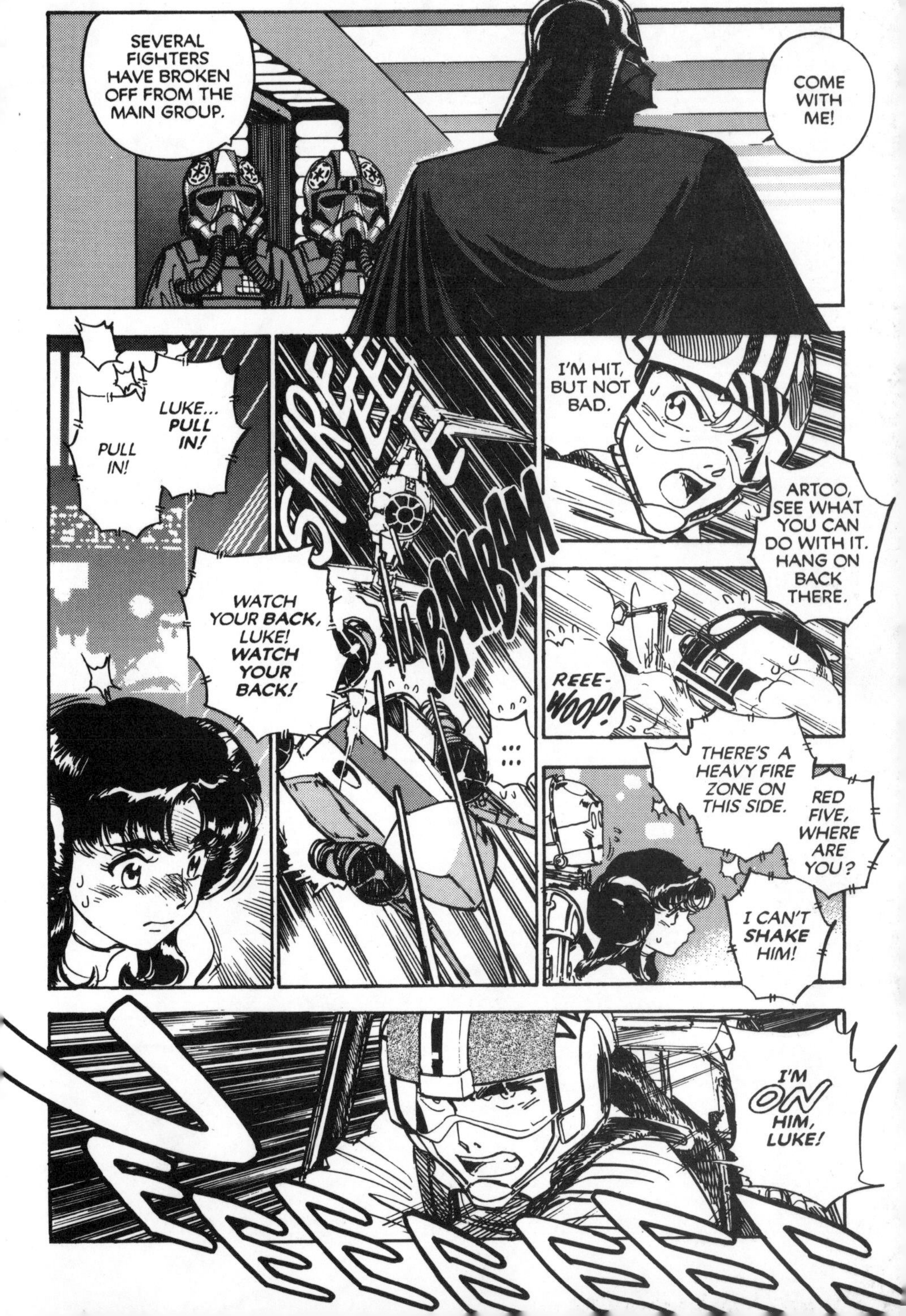

SEVERAL FIGHTERS HAVE BROKEN OFF FROM THE MAIN GROUP.
COME WITH ME!
LUKE... PULL IN!
PULL IN!
WATCH YOUR BACK, LUKE! WATCH YOUR BACK!
SHREEEE
BAMBAM
...
I'M HIT, BUT NOT BAD.
ARTOO, SEE WHAT YOU CAN DO WITH IT. HANG ON BACK THERE.
REEE-WOOP!
THERE'S A HEAVY FIRE ZONE ON THIS SIDE.
RED FIVE, WHERE ARE YOU?
I CAN'T SHAKE HIM!
I'M ON HIM, LUKE!

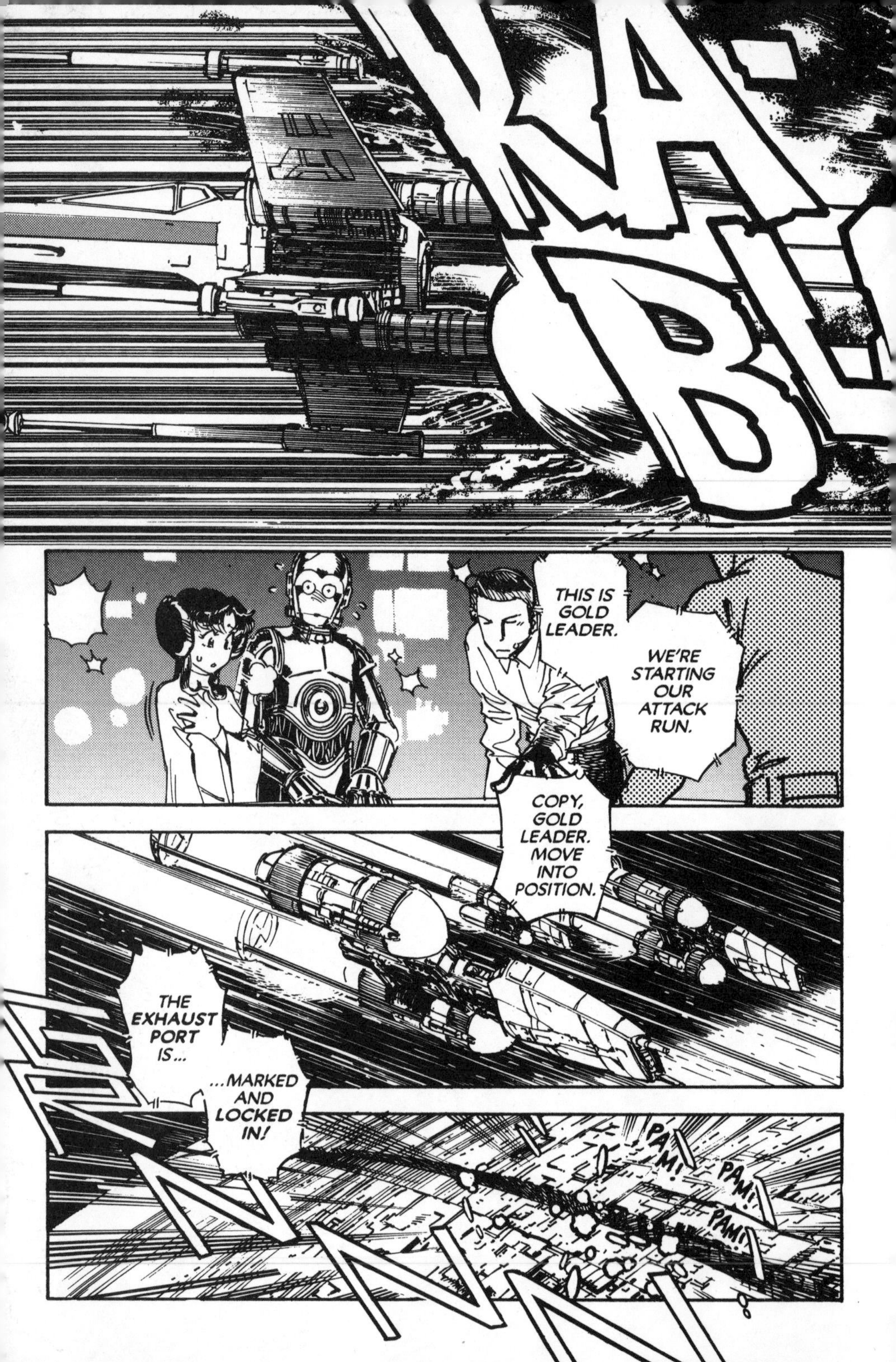
KA-
BL
THIS IS GOLD LEADER.
WE'RE STARTING OUR ATTACK RUN.
COPY, GOLD LEADER. MOVE INTO POSITION.
THE EXHAUST PORT IS...
...MARKED AND LOCKED IN!
PAM!
PAM!
PAM!
PAM!

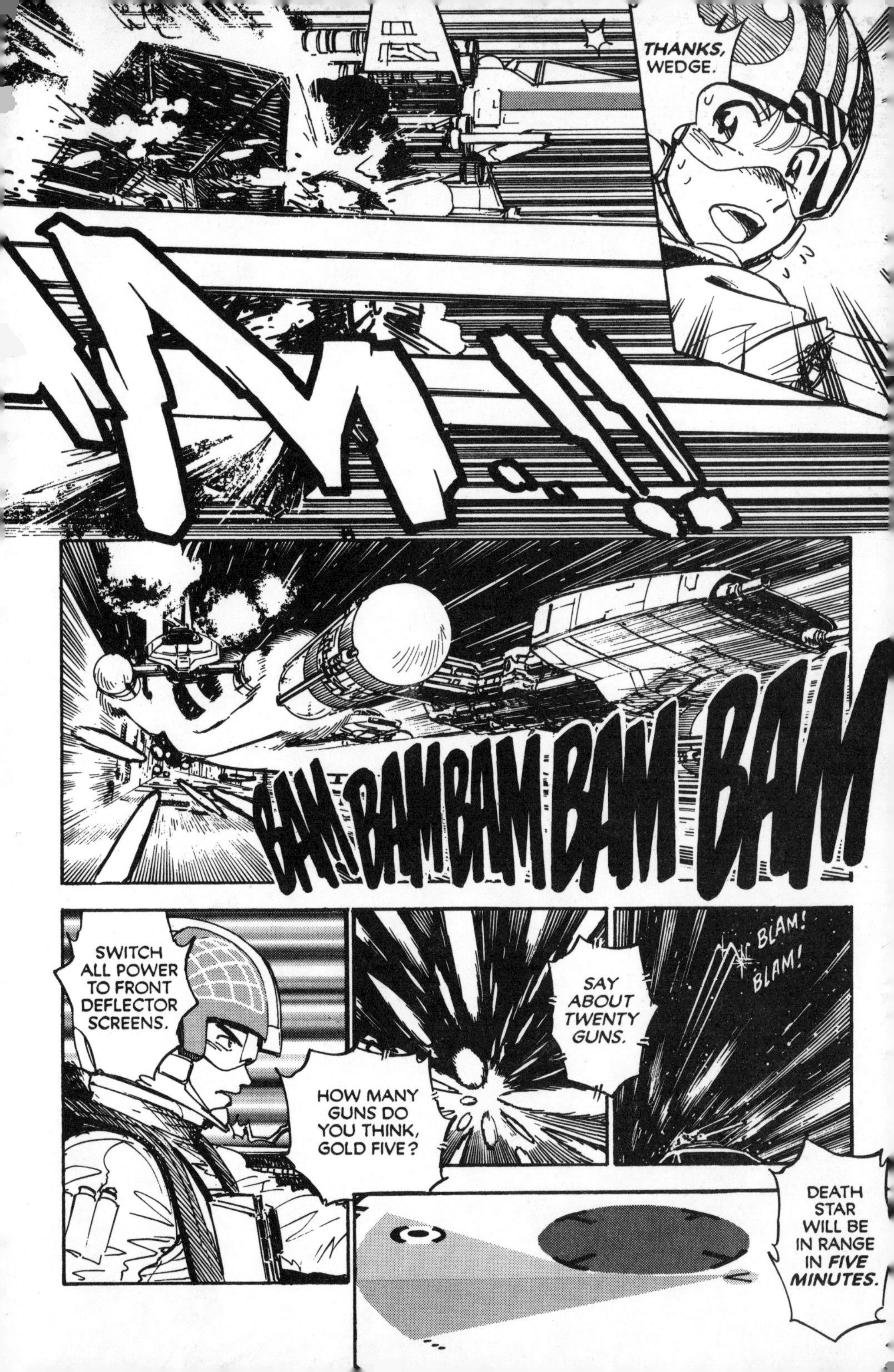
THANKS, WEDGE.
BAM BAM BAM BAM BAM
SWITCH ALL POWER TO FRONT DEFLECTOR SCREENS.
HOW MANY GUNS DO YOU THINK, GOLD FIVE?
SAY ABOUT TWENTY GUNS.
BLAM!
BLAM!
DEATH STAR WILL BE IN RANGE IN *FIVE MINUTES.*

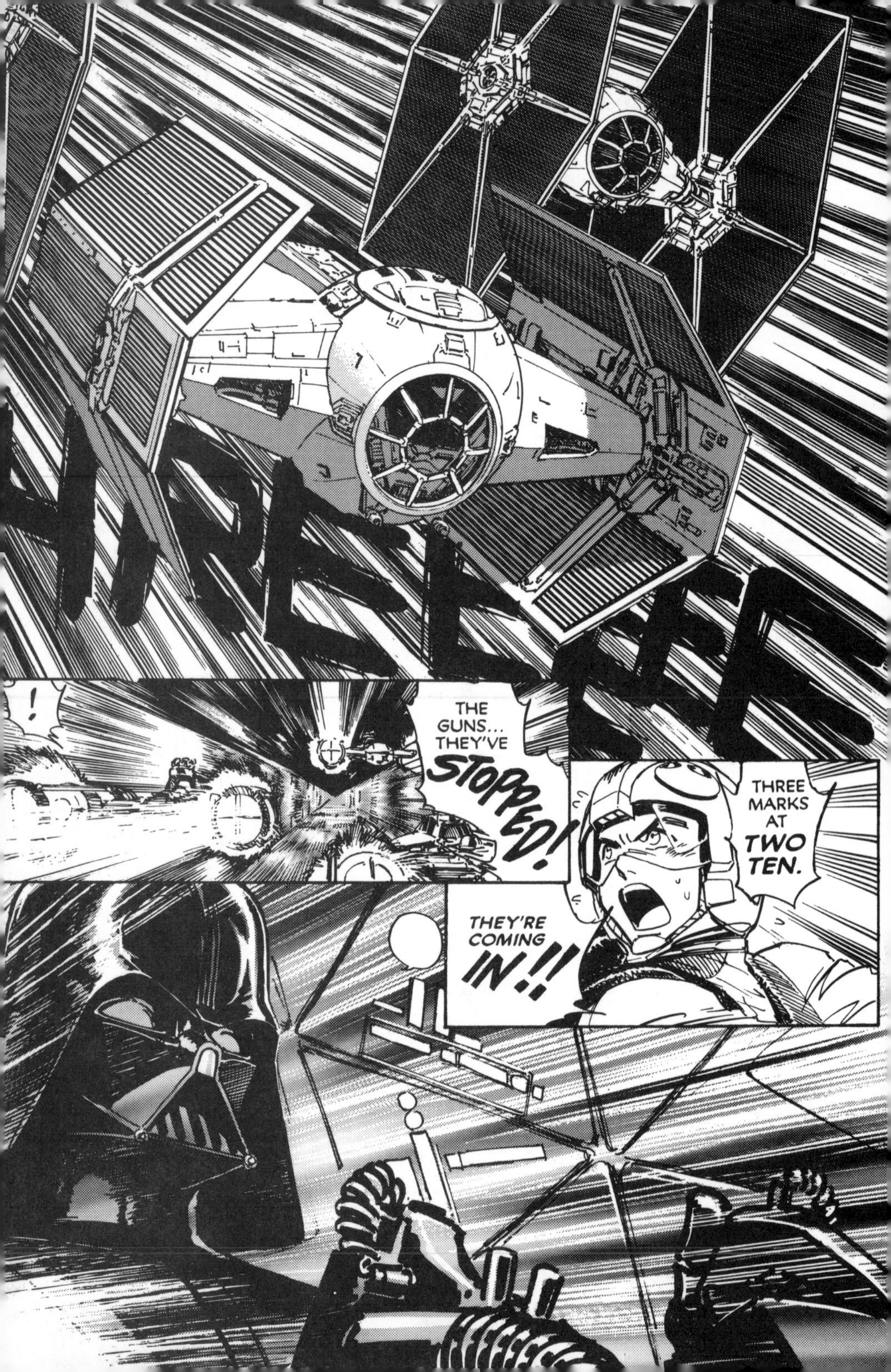
!
THE GUNS... THEY'VE STOPPED!
THREE MARKS AT TWO TEN.
THEY'RE COMING IN!!

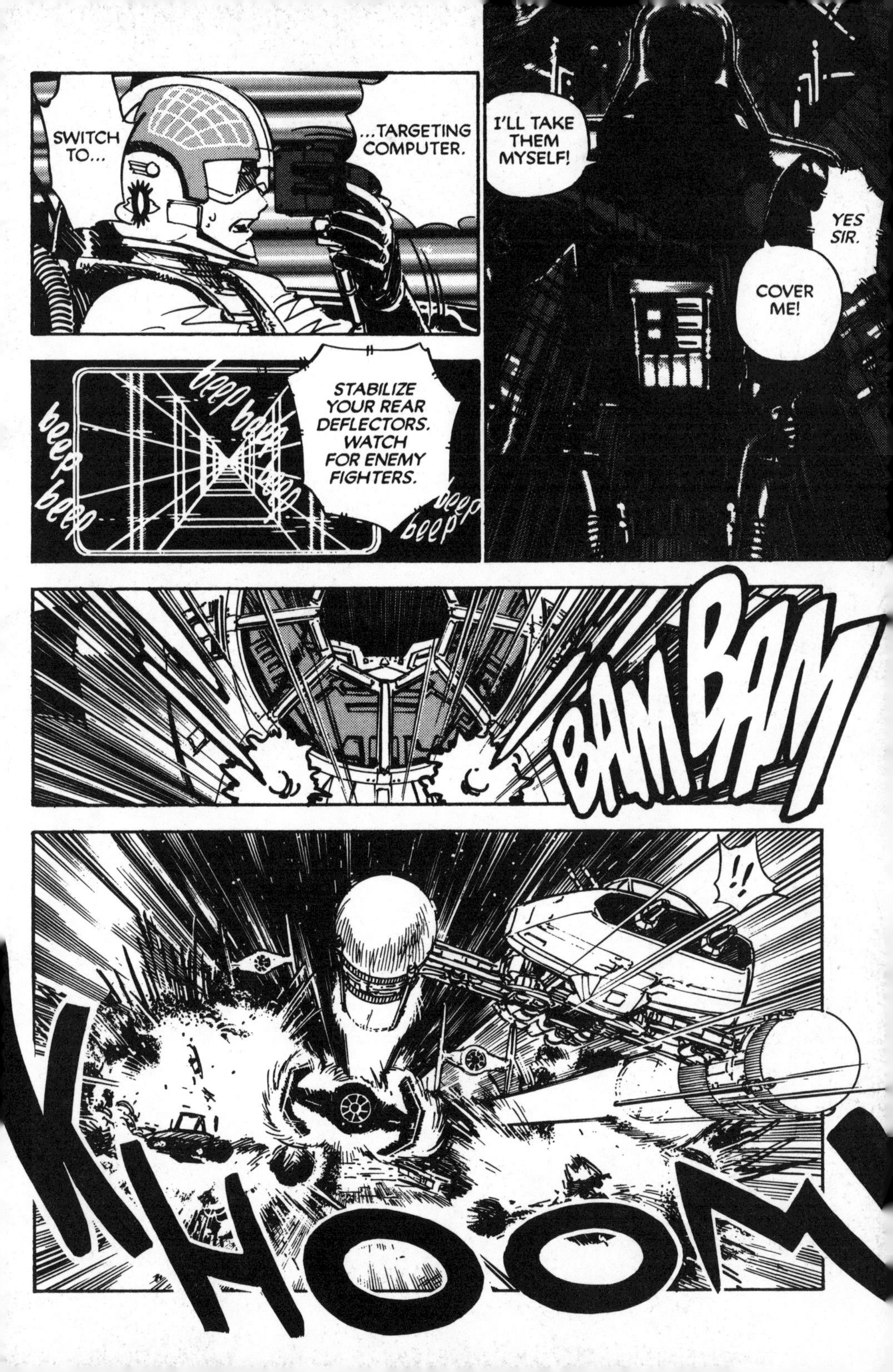
SWITCH TO...
...TARGETING COMPUTER.
I'LL TAKE THEM MYSELF!
YES SIR.
COVER ME!
STABILIZE YOUR REAR DEFLECTORS. WATCH FOR ENEMY FIGHTERS.
beep beep
beep beep
beep beep
beep beep
BAM BAM
!!
WHOOM

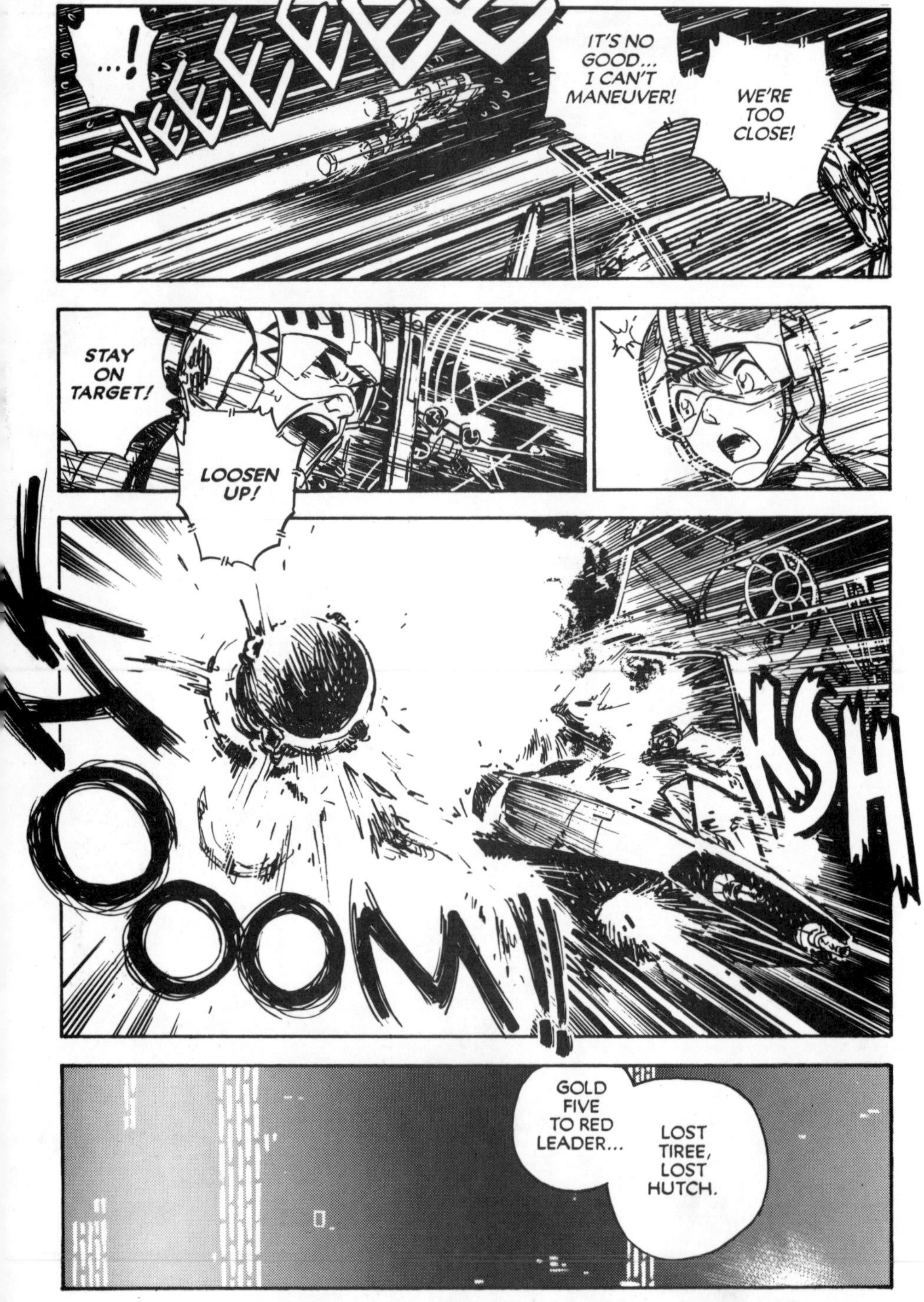
...!
VEEEEEE
IT'S NO GOOD... I CAN'T MANEUVER!
WE'RE TOO CLOSE!
STAY ON TARGET!
LOOSEN UP!
OOOM!!
KSH
GOLD FIVE TO RED LEADER...
LOST TIREE, LOST HUTCH.

WE'VE ANALYZED THEIR ATTACK, SIR-- --AND THERE IS A DANGER.

SHOULD I HAVE YOUR SHIP STANDING BY?

EVAC-UATE?

IN OUR MOMENT OF *TRIUMPH?*

I THINK YOU *OVER-ESTIMATE* THEIR *CHANCES!*

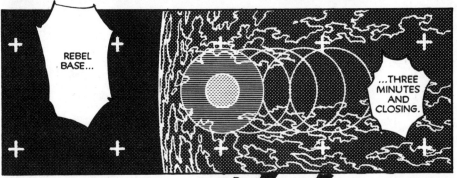

REBEL BASE...

...THREE MINUTES AND CLOSING.

RED BOYS, THIS IS RED LEADER.

RENDEZVOUS AT MARK SIX POINT ONE.

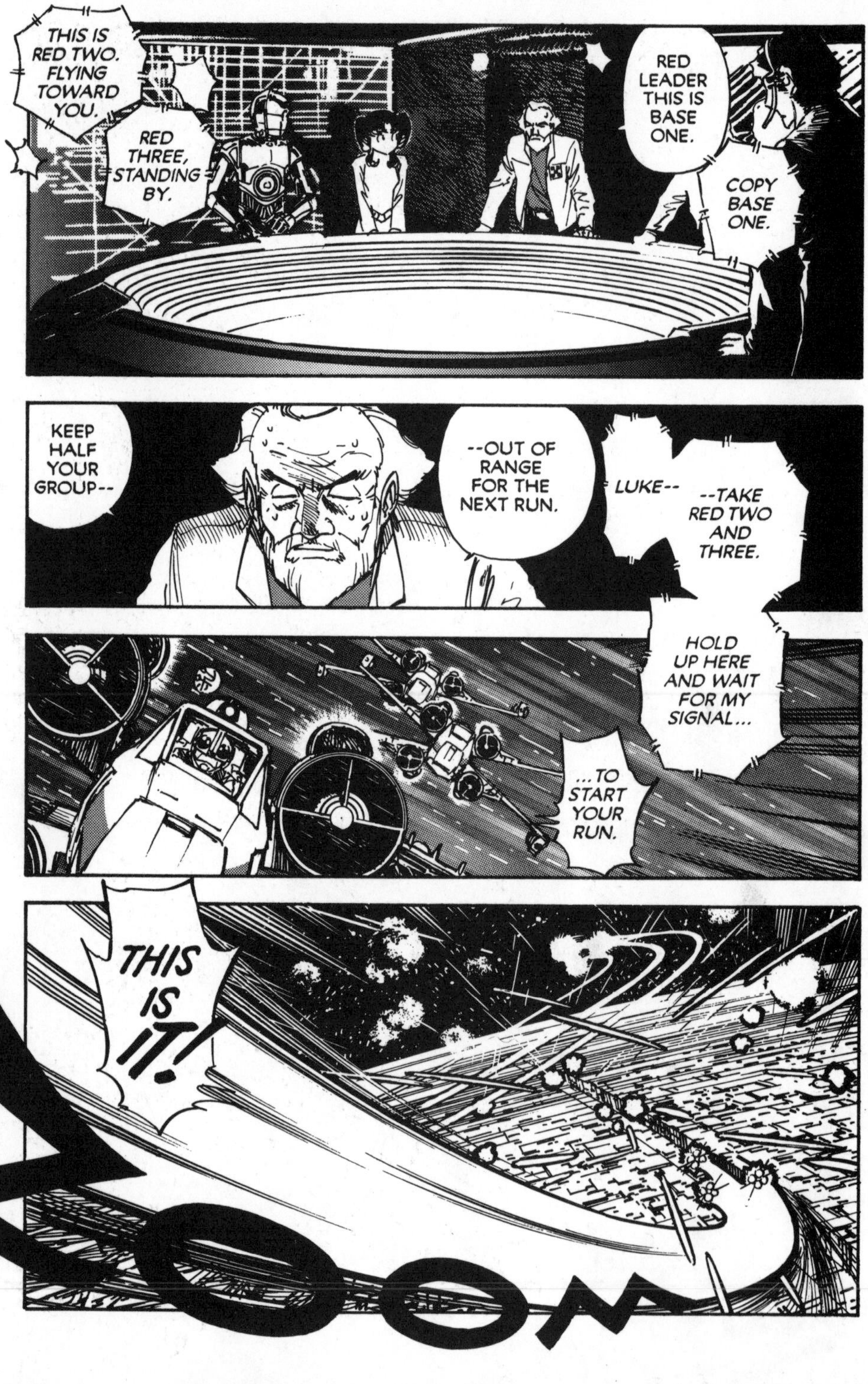
THIS IS RED TWO. FLYING TOWARD YOU.
RED THREE, STANDING BY.
RED LEADER THIS IS BASE ONE.
COPY BASE ONE.
KEEP HALF YOUR GROUP--
--OUT OF RANGE FOR THE NEXT RUN.
LUKE--
--TAKE RED TWO AND THREE.
HOLD UP HERE AND WAIT FOR MY SIGNAL...
...TO START YOUR RUN.
THIS IS IT!
OOM

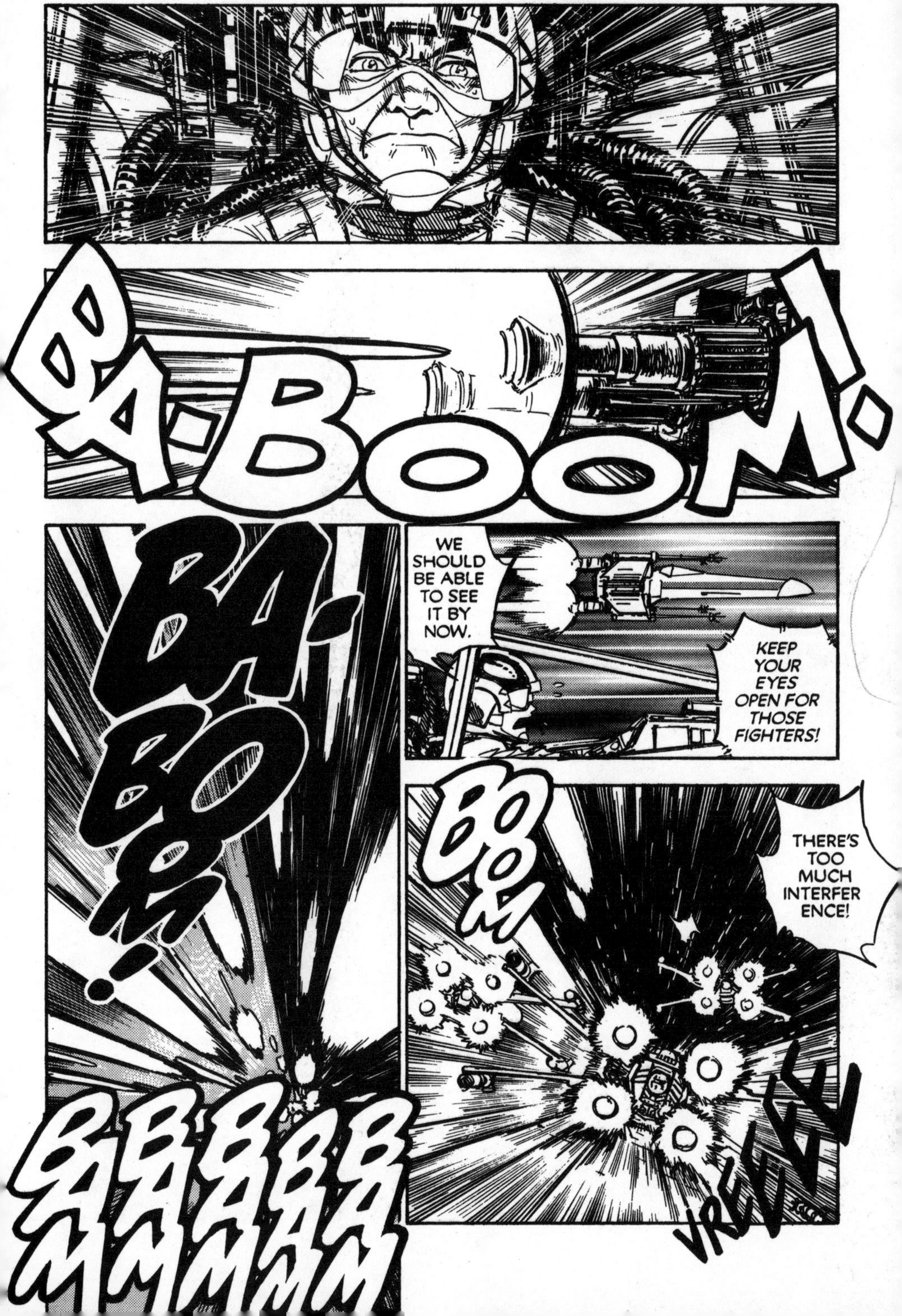
BA-BOOM!
BA-BOOM!
WE SHOULD BE ABLE TO SEE IT BY NOW.
KEEP YOUR EYES OPEN FOR THOSE FIGHTERS!
BOOM
THERE'S TOO MUCH INTERFERENCE!
BBBBBB AAAAAA MMMMMM
VREEE

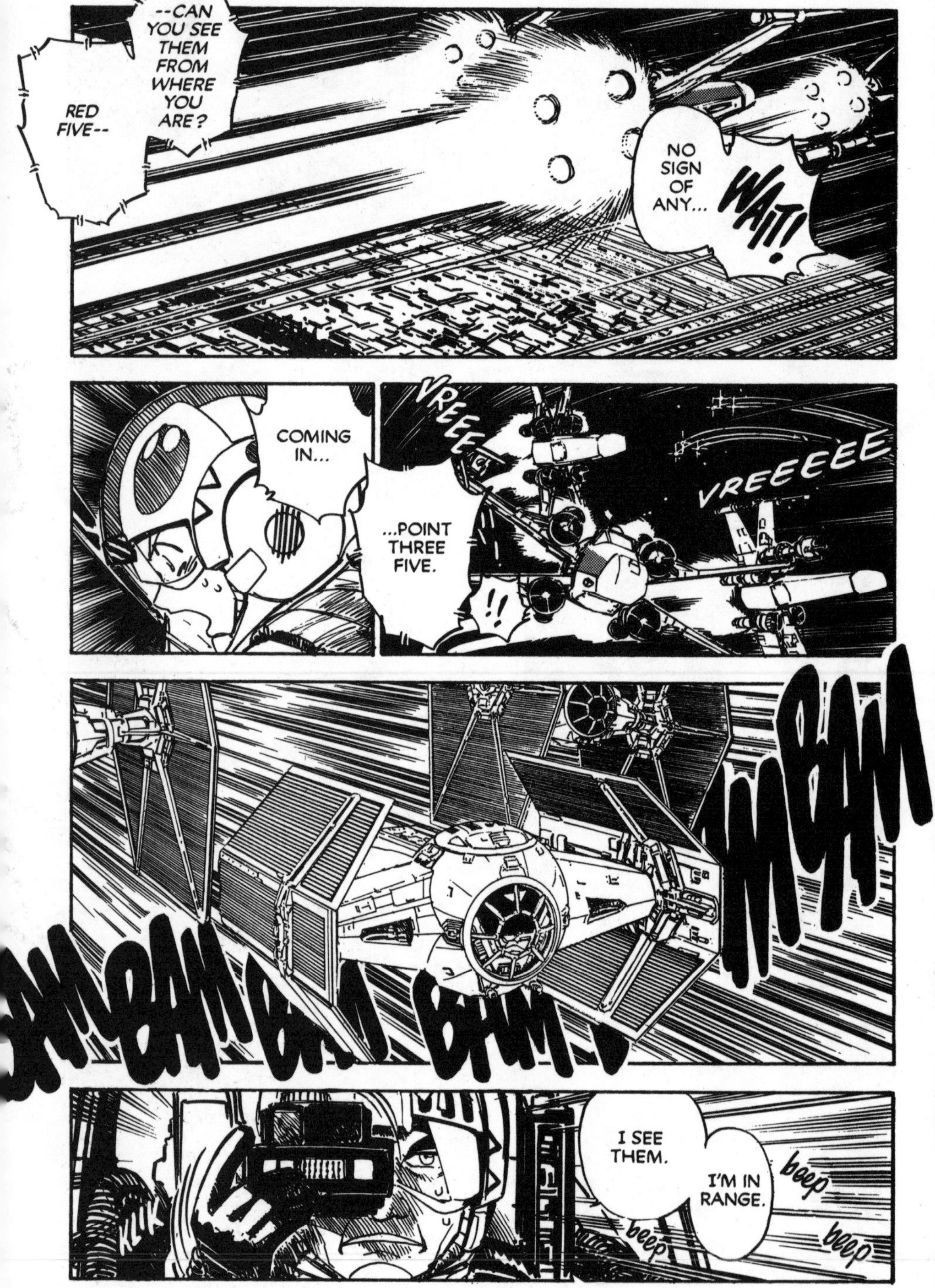
RED FIVE--
--CAN YOU SEE THEM FROM WHERE YOU ARE?
NO SIGN OF ANY...
WAIT!
COMING IN...
...POINT THREE FIVE.
!!
VREEE
VREEEEEE
BAM BAM
BAM BAM BAM BAM BAM
I SEE THEM.
I'M IN RANGE.
KLIK
beep
beep
beep

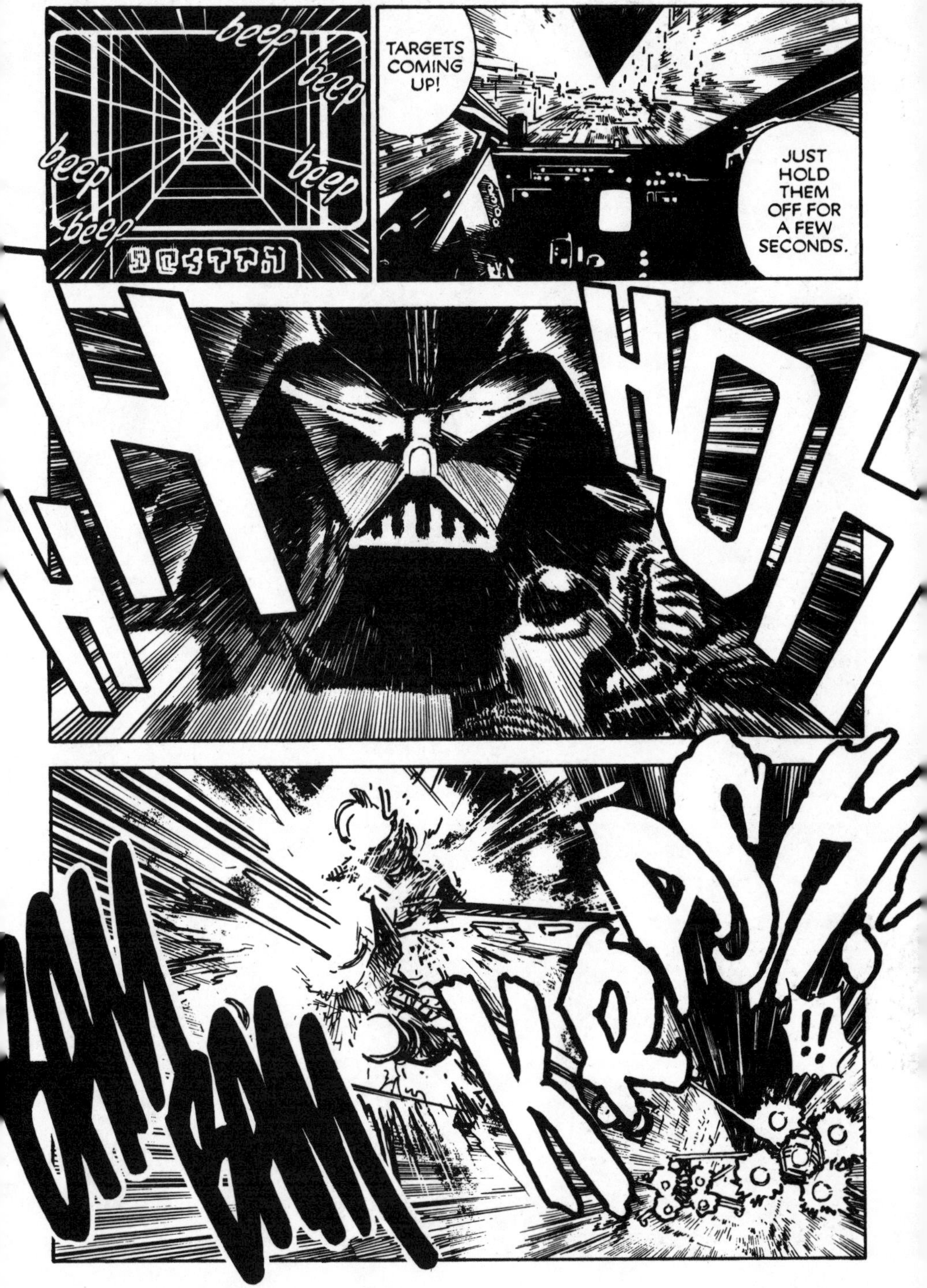
beep
beep
beep
beep
beep
TARGETS COMING UP!
JUST HOLD THEM OFF FOR A FEW SECONDS.
!!

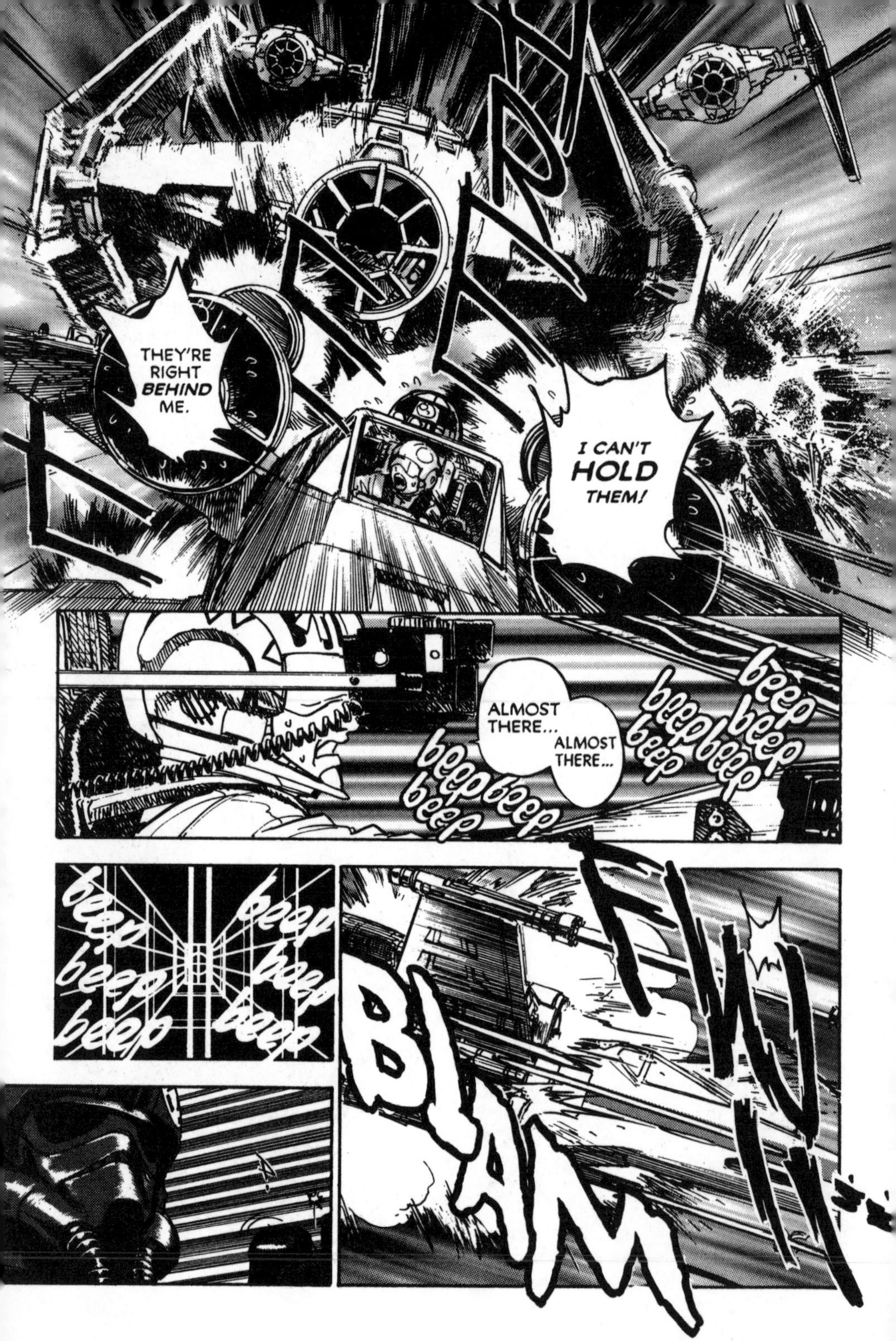
THEY'RE RIGHT *BEHIND* ME.
I CAN'T **HOLD** THEM!
ALMOST THERE...
ALMOST THERE...
beep beep beep beep
beep beep beep
beep beep beep
beep beep beep
BLAM

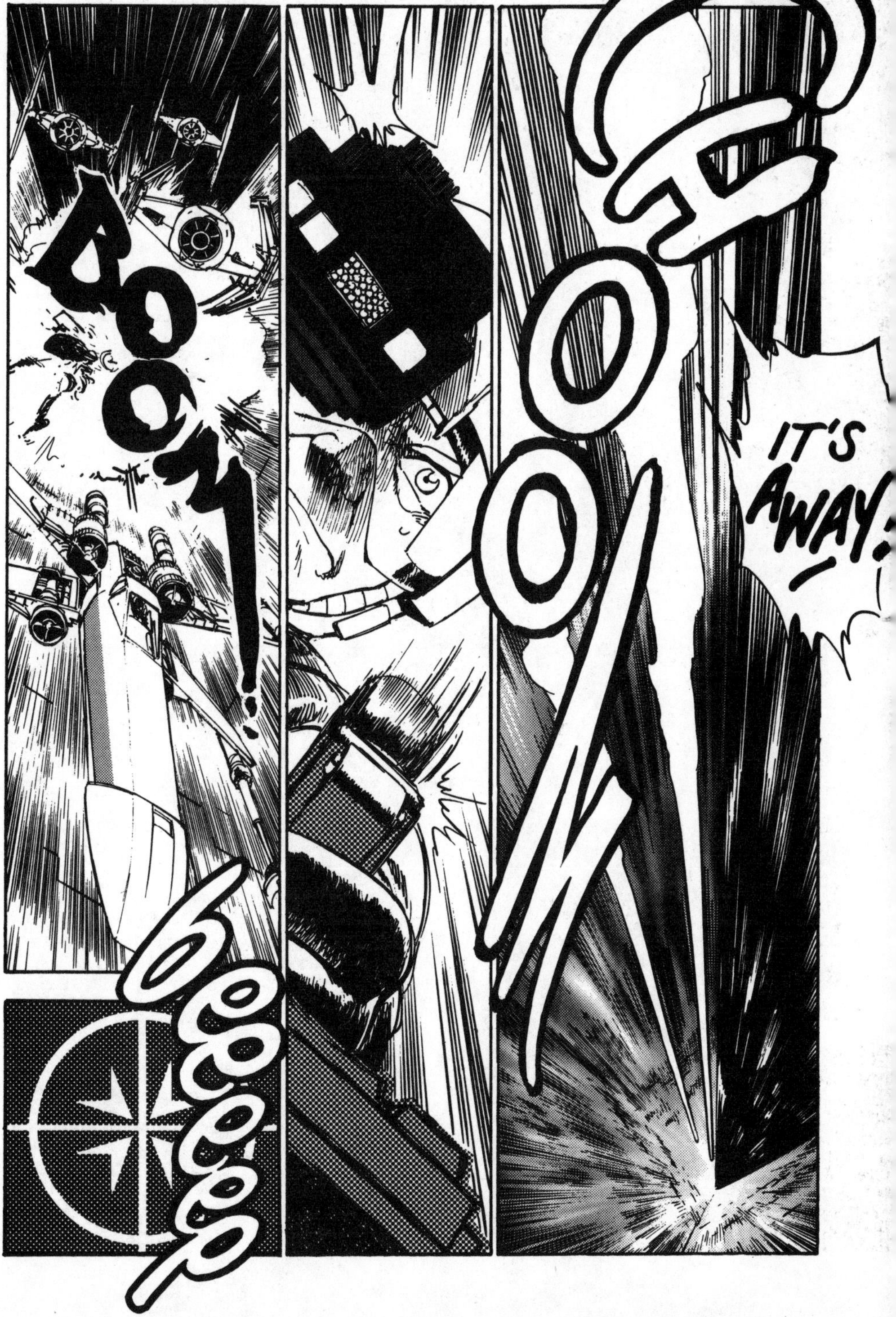
BOOM!
IT'S AWAY!

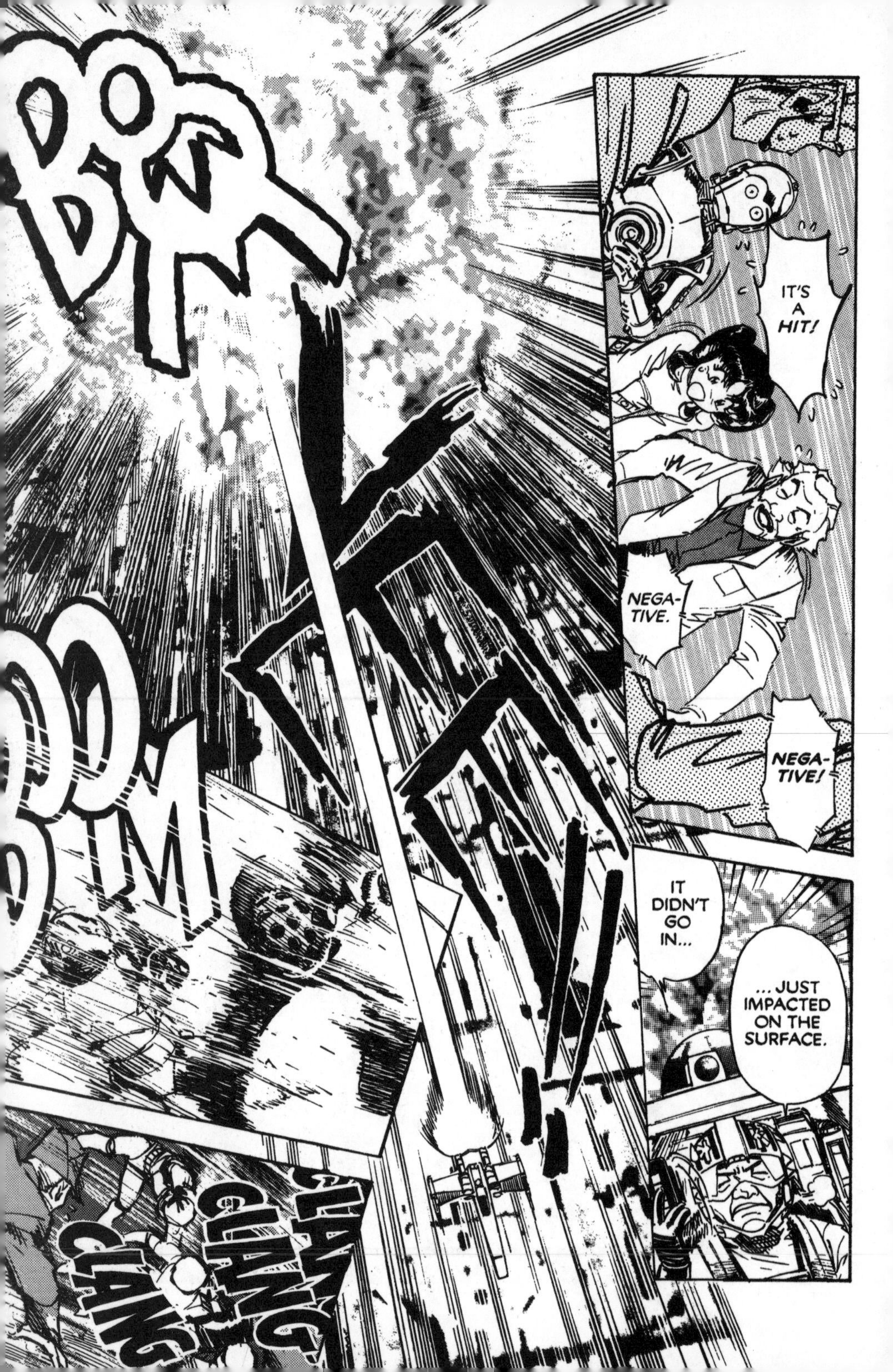
IT'S A HIT!
NEGA-TIVE.
NEGA-TIVE!
IT DIDN'T GO IN...
... JUST IMPACTED ON THE SURFACE.
CLANG
CLANG
CLANG

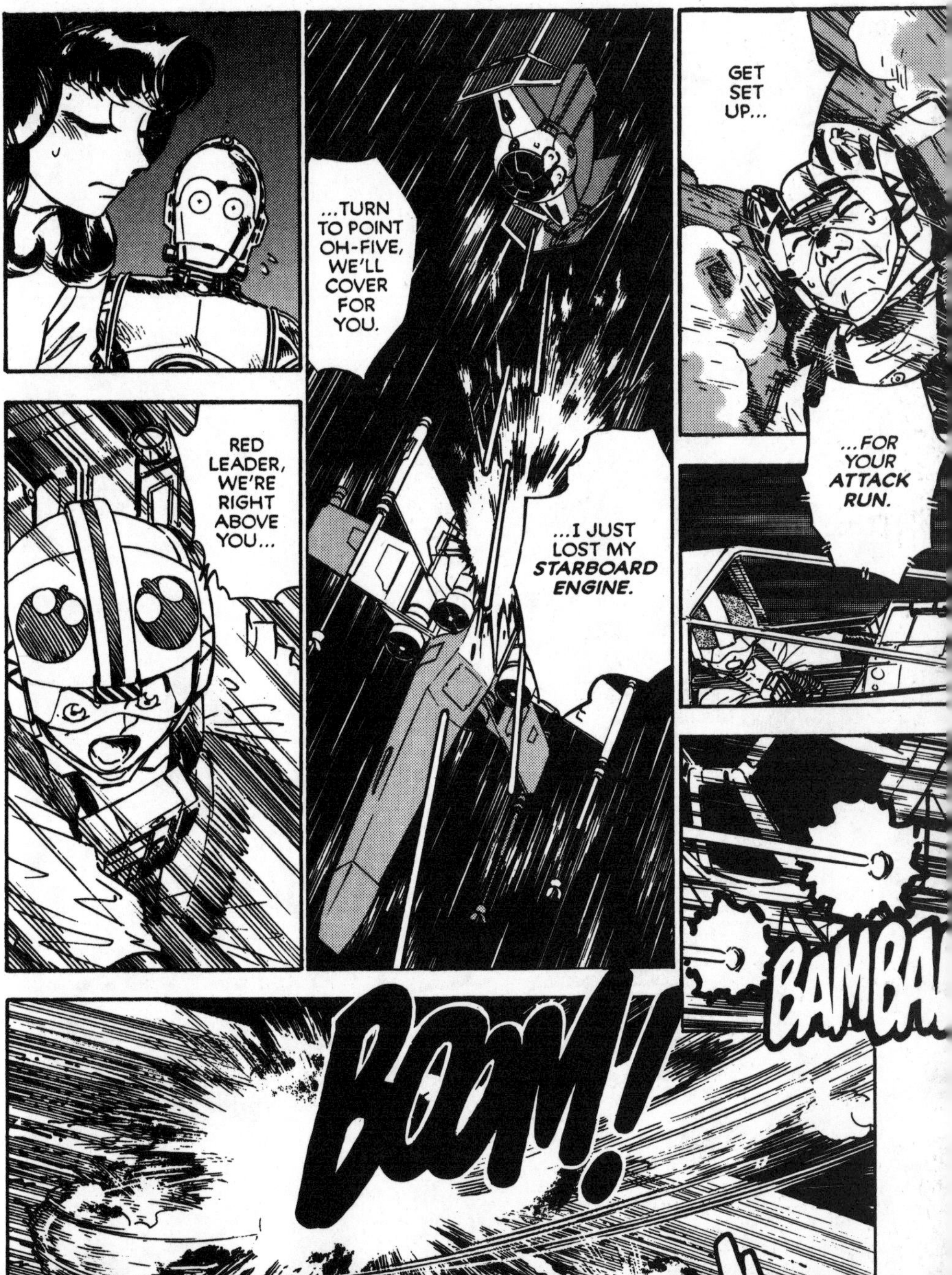
RED LEADER, WE'RE RIGHT ABOVE YOU...
...TURN TO POINT OH-FIVE, WE'LL COVER FOR YOU.
...I JUST LOST MY *STARBOARD* ENGINE.
GET SET UP...
...FOR YOUR **ATTACK RUN.**
BAMBA
BOOM!
BOOM

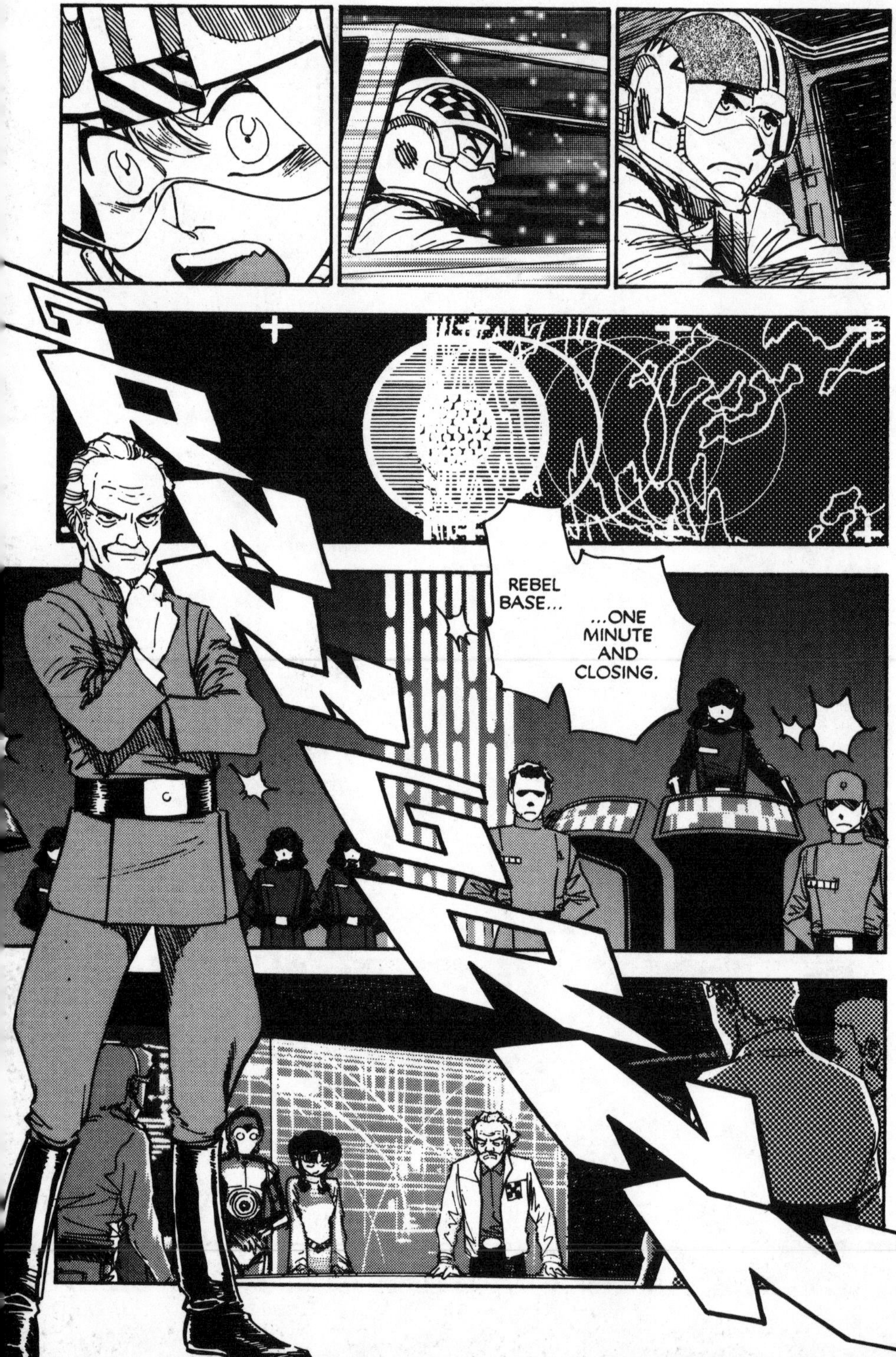
REBEL BASE...
...ONE MINUTE AND CLOSING.

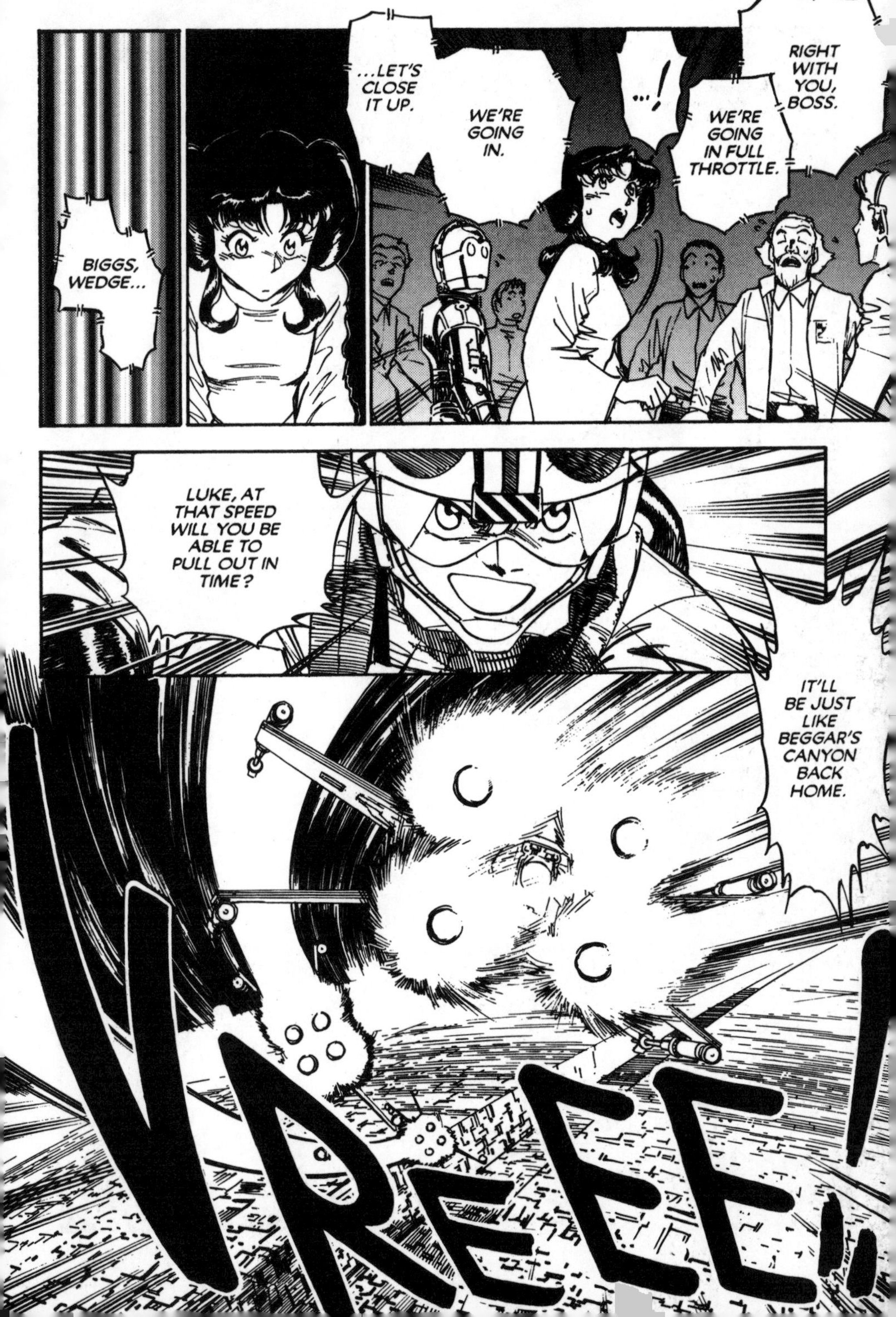
BIGGS, WEDGE...
...LET'S CLOSE IT UP.
WE'RE GOING IN.
...!
WE'RE GOING IN FULL THROTTLE.
RIGHT WITH YOU, BOSS.
LUKE, AT THAT SPEED WILL YOU BE ABLE TO PULL OUT IN TIME?
IT'LL BE JUST LIKE BEGGAR'S CANYON BACK HOME.
VREEE!!

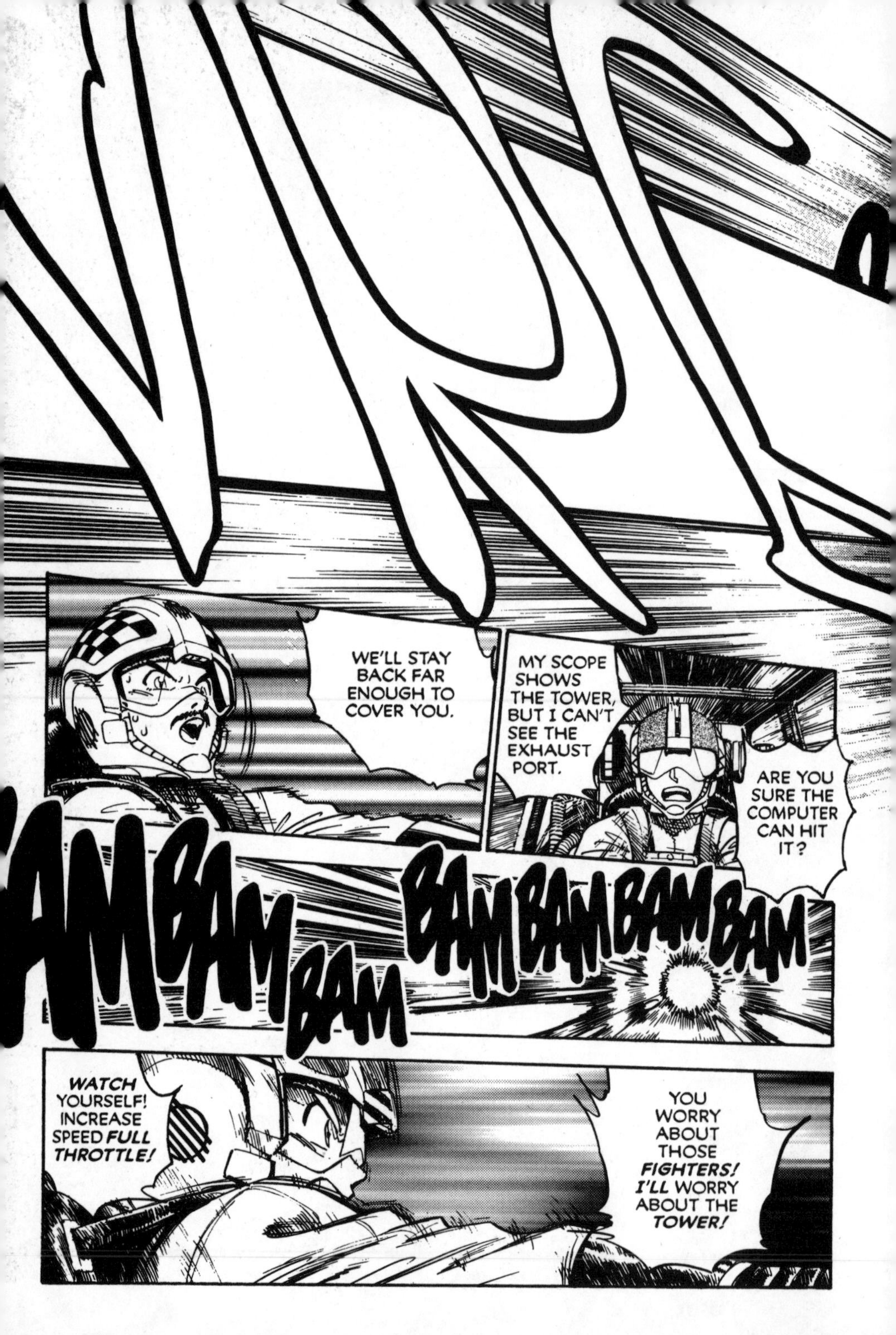

WE'LL STAY BACK FAR ENOUGH TO COVER YOU.
MY SCOPE SHOWS THE TOWER, BUT I CAN'T SEE THE EXHAUST PORT.
ARE YOU SURE THE COMPUTER CAN HIT IT?
BAM BAM BAM BAM BAM BAM
WATCH YOURSELF! INCREASE SPEED FULL THROTTLE!
YOU WORRY ABOUT THOSE FIGHTERS! I'LL WORRY ABOUT THE TOWER!

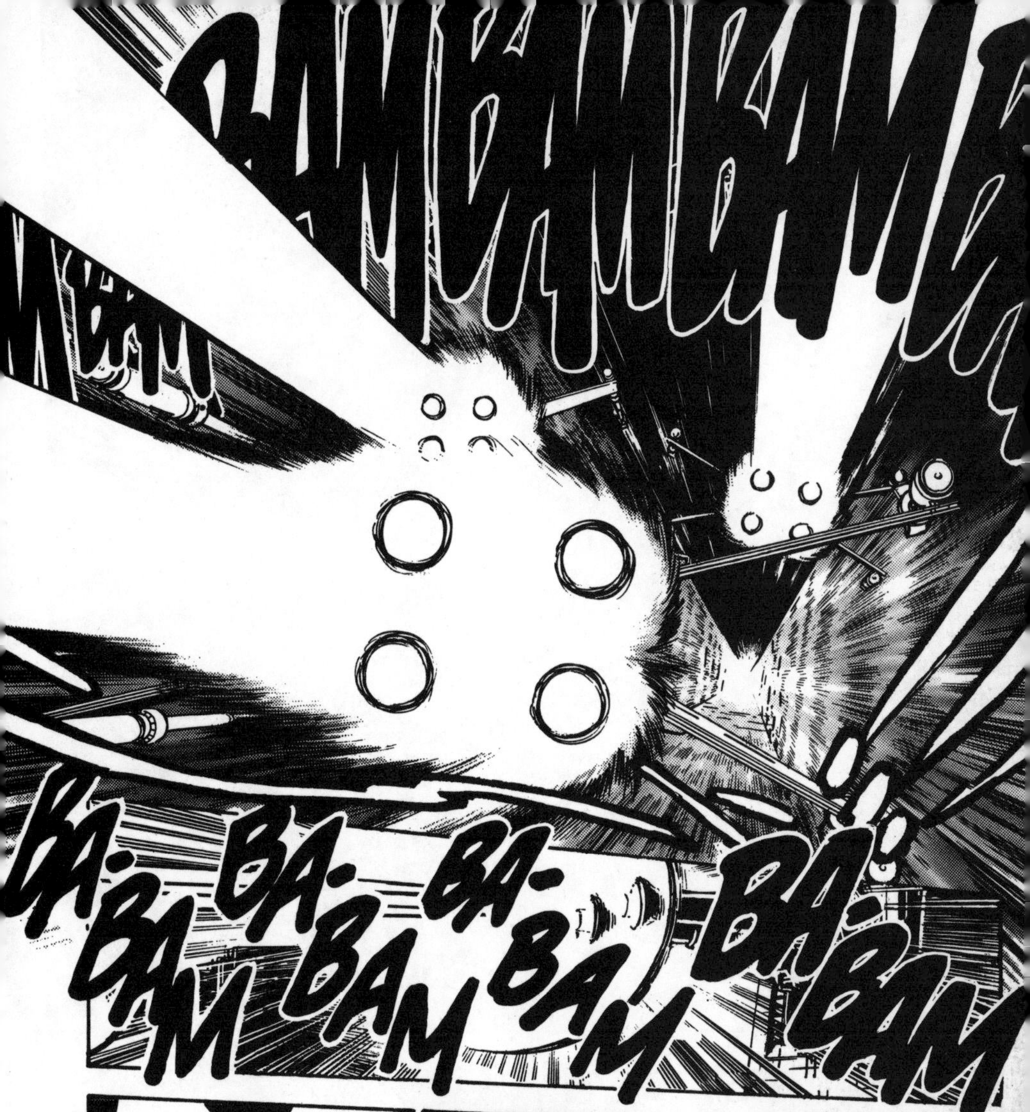
BA-BAM
BA-BAM
BA-BAM
BA-BAM

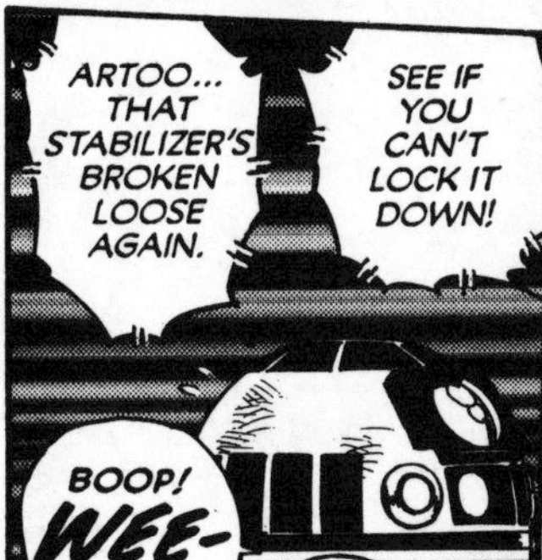
ARTOO... THAT STABILIZER'S BROKEN LOOSE AGAIN.
SEE IF YOU CAN'T LOCK IT DOWN!
BOOP! WEE-OOP!

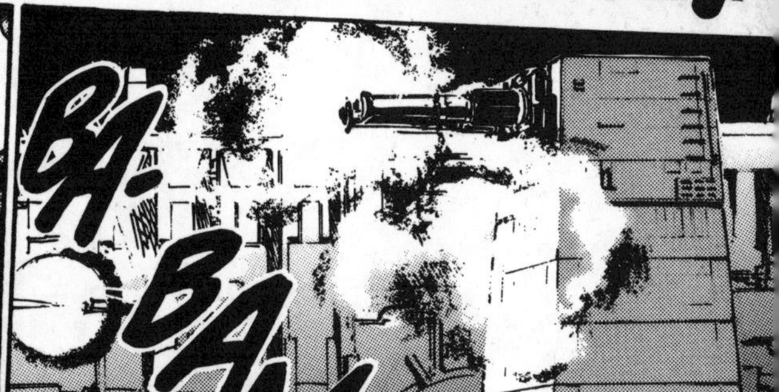
BA-BAM

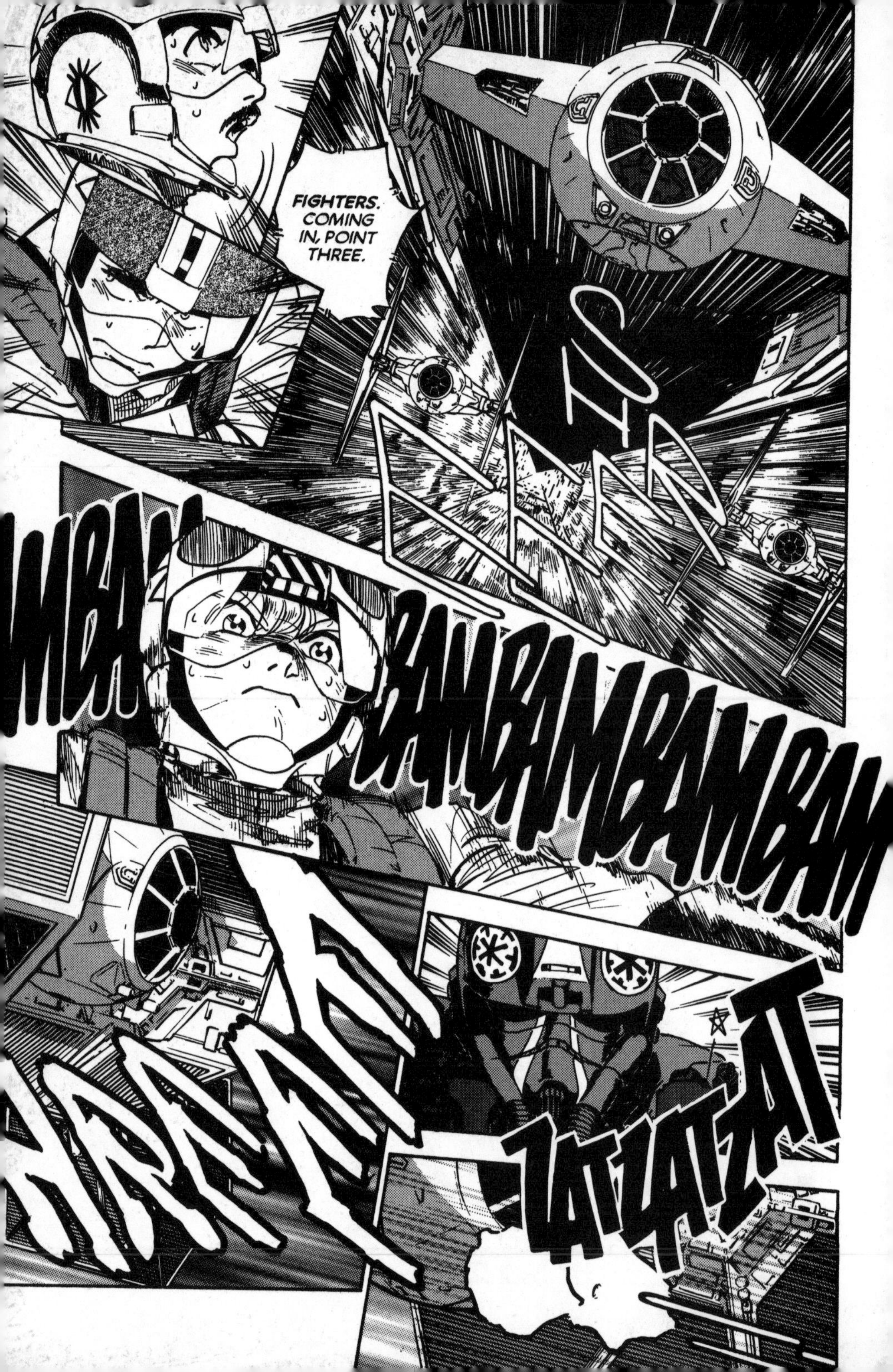
FIGHTERS. COMING IN, POINT THREE.
BAMBAMBAMBAMBAM
ZATZATZAT

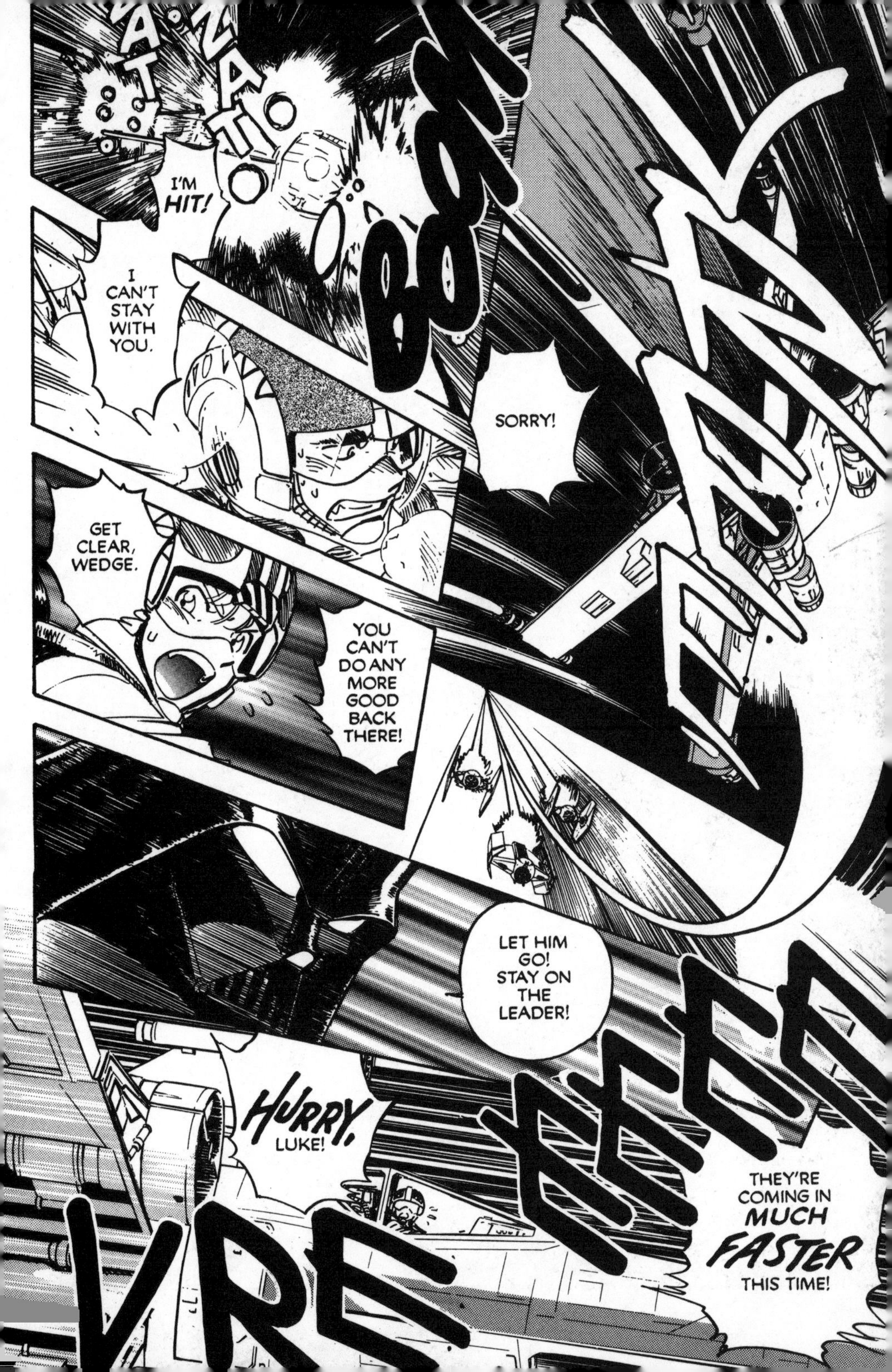
I'M HIT!
BOOM
SORRY!
I CAN'T STAY WITH YOU.
GET CLEAR, WEDGE.
YOU CAN'T DO ANY MORE GOOD BACK THERE!
LET HIM GO! STAY ON THE LEADER!
HURRY, LUKE!
THEY'RE COMING IN MUCH FASTER THIS TIME!

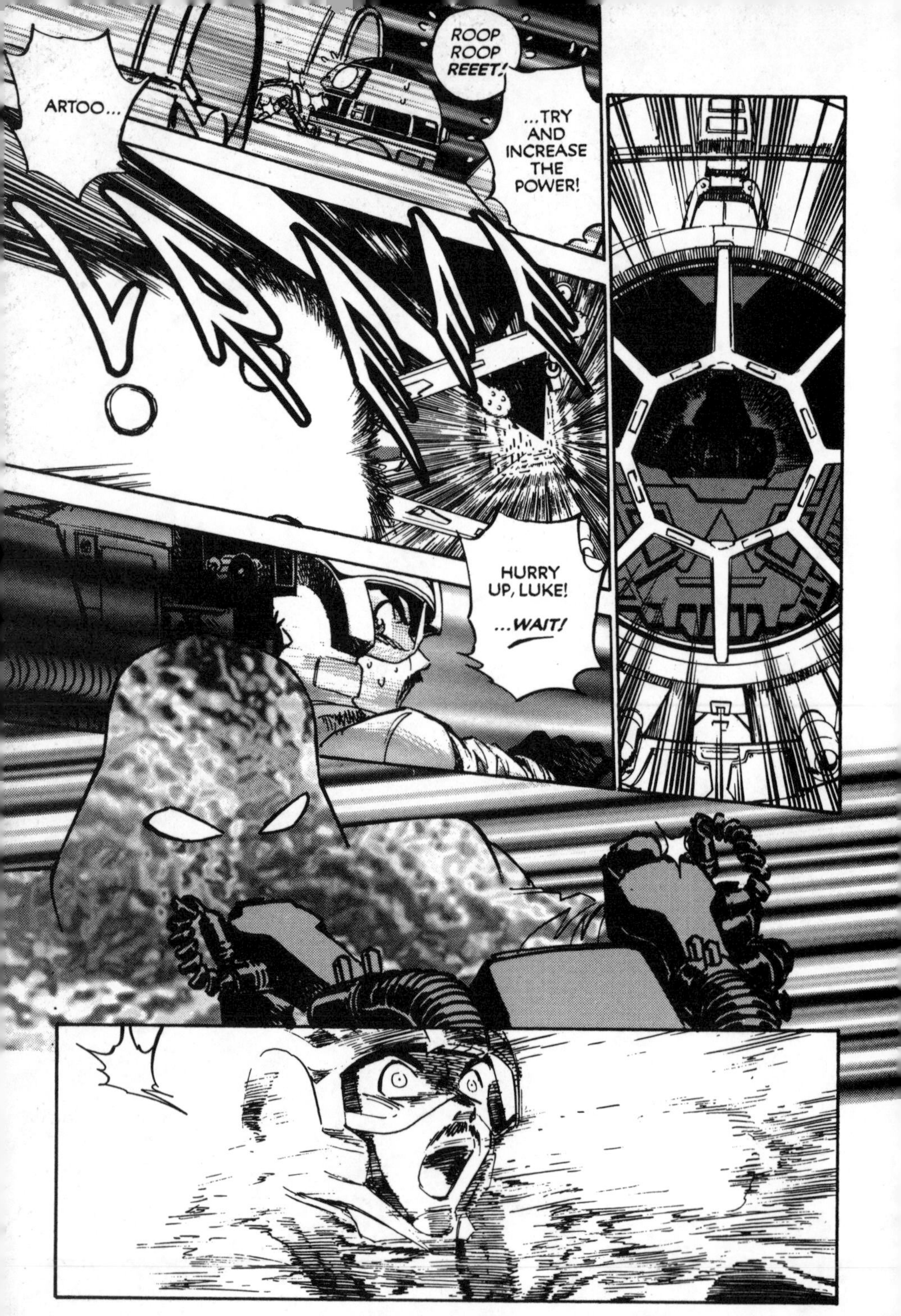
ARTOO...
ROOP ROOP REEET!
...TRY AND INCREASE THE POWER!
HURRY UP, LUKE!
...WAIT!

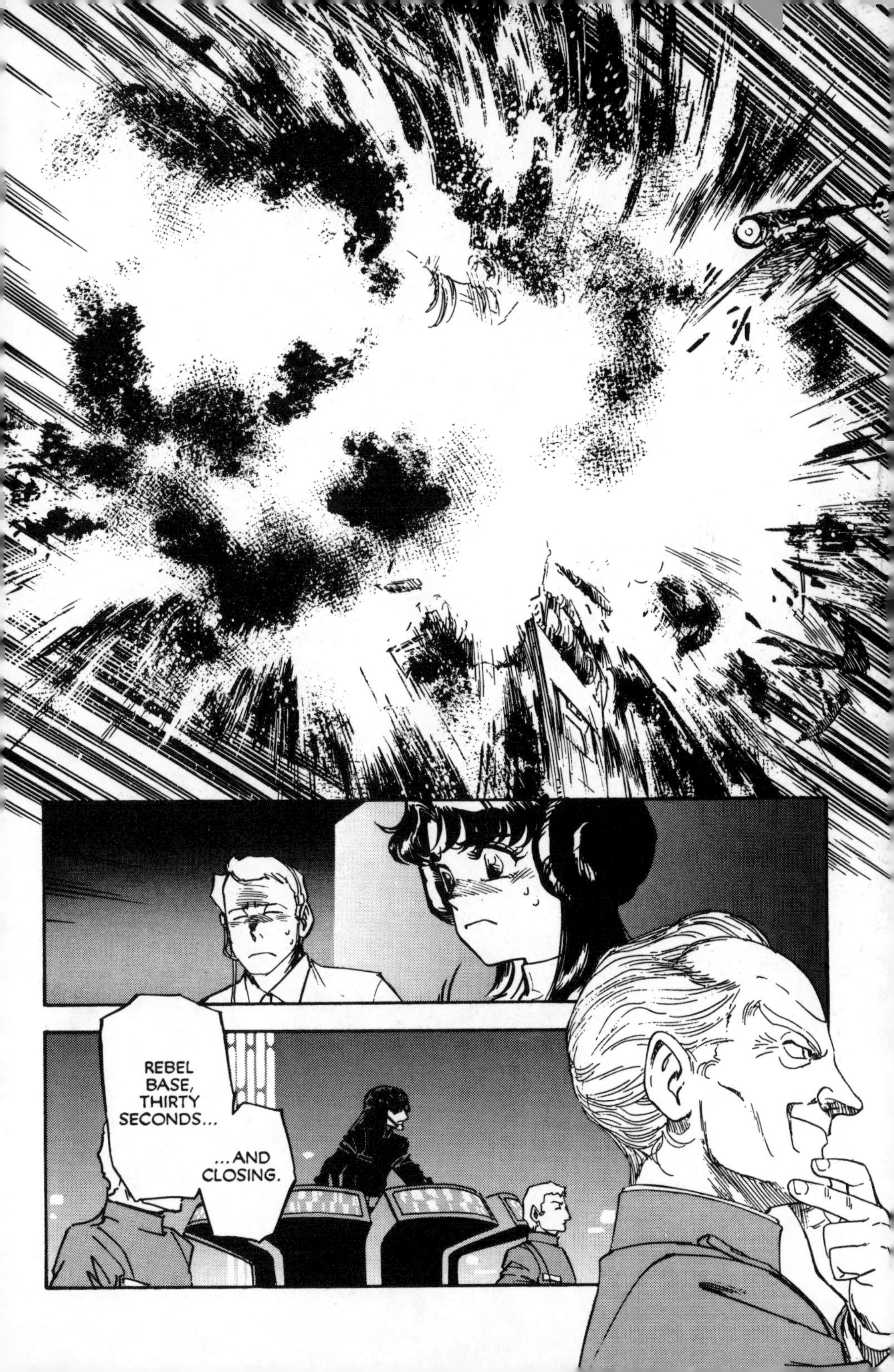
REBEL BASE, THIRTY SECONDS...
...AND CLOSING.

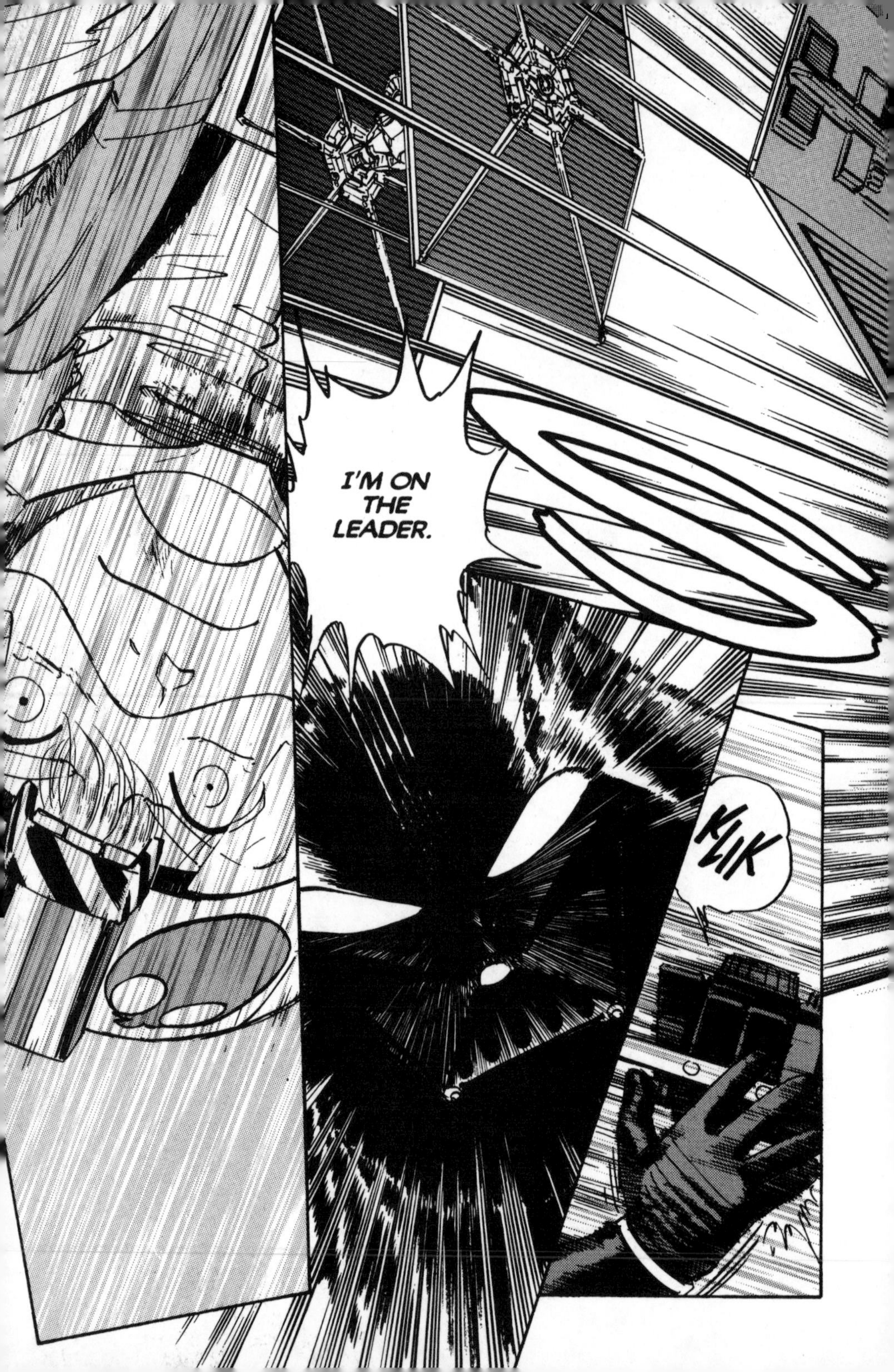
I'M ON THE LEADER.
KLIK

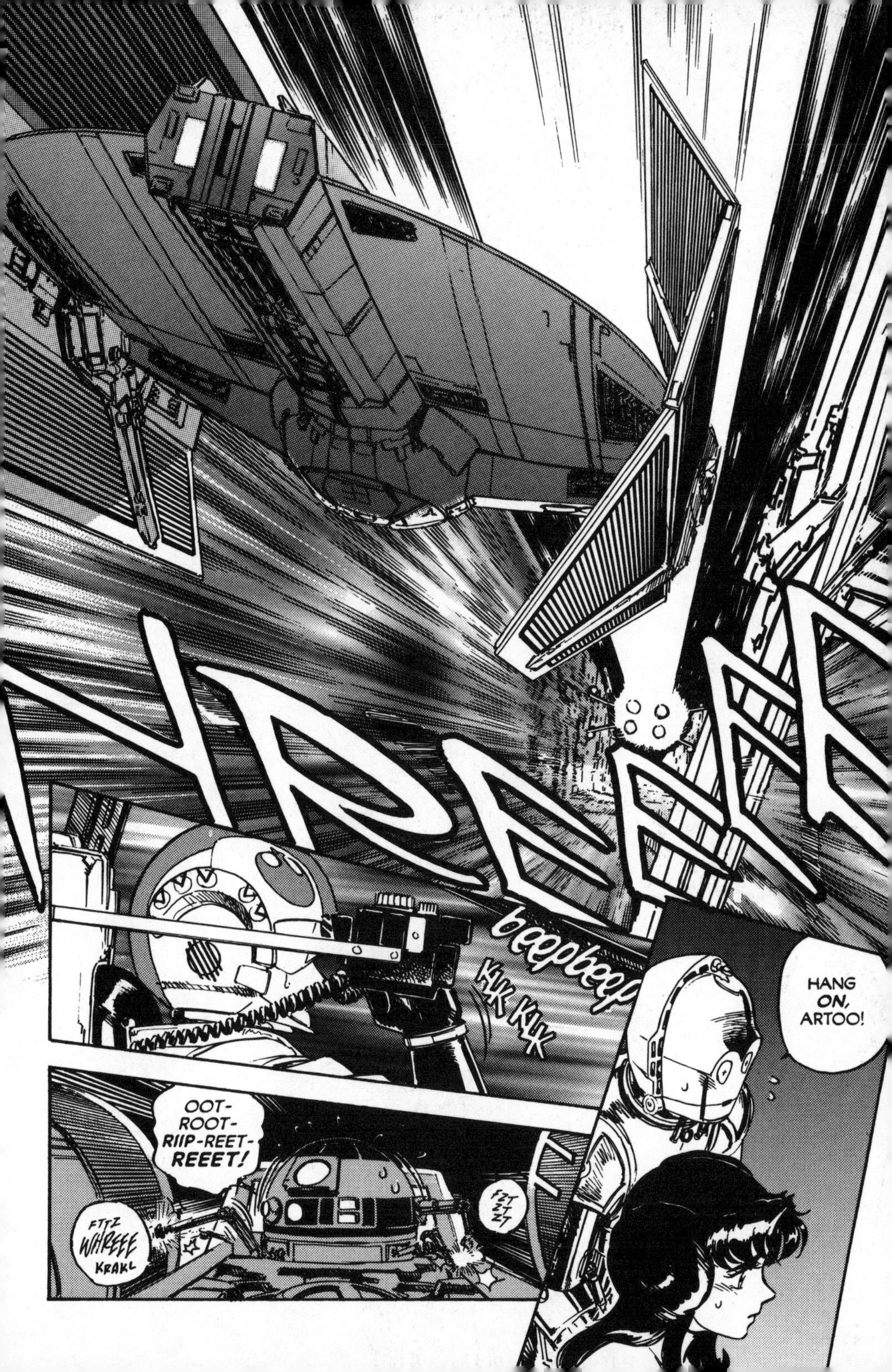
KREEEE
beepbeep
KLIK KLIK
HANG ON, ARTOO!
OOT-ROOT-RIIP-REET-REEET!
FTTZ WHREEE KRAKL
FZT ZT ZT

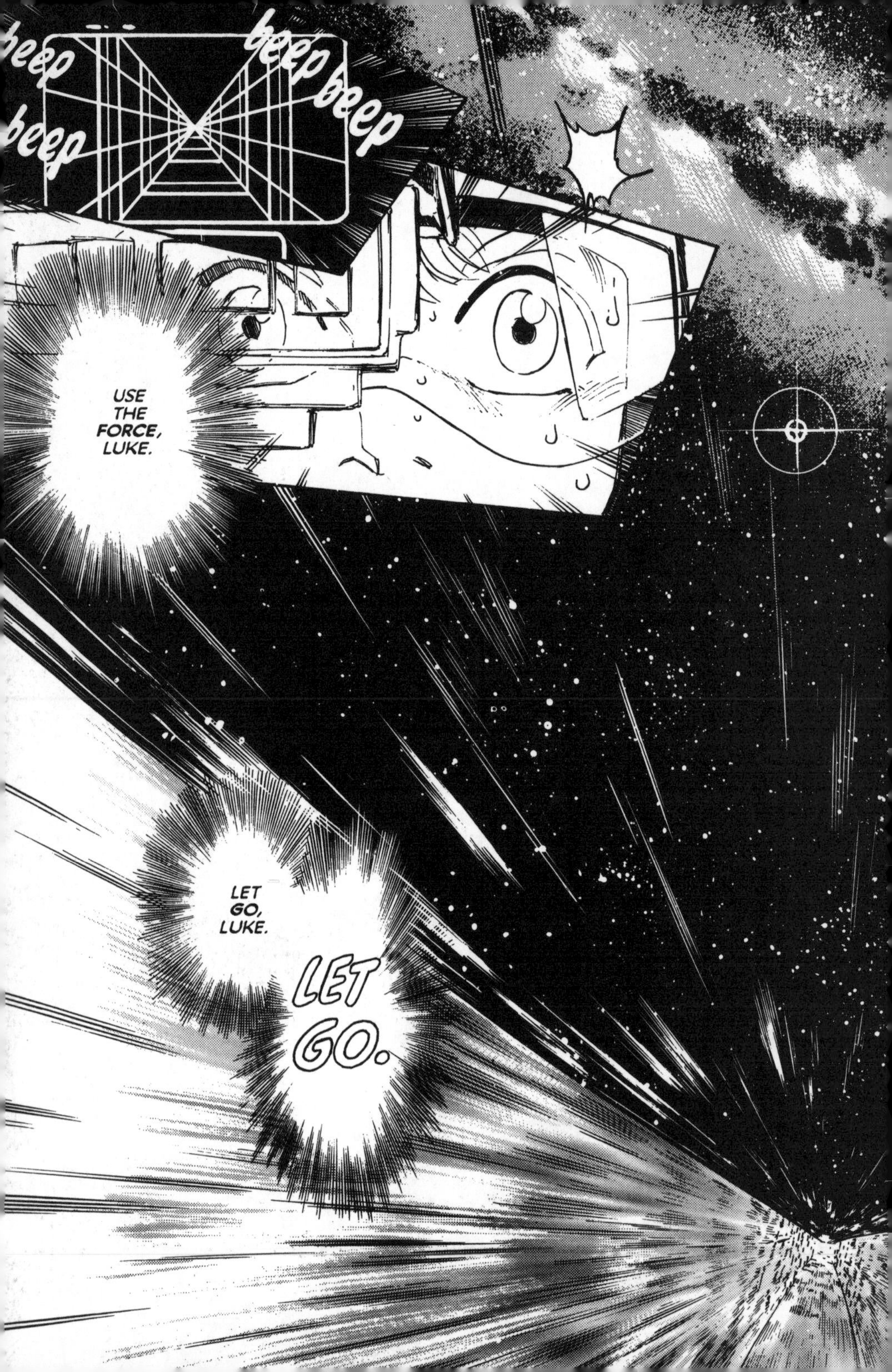
beep
beep
beep beep
USE THE FORCE, LUKE.
LET GO, LUKE.
LET GO.

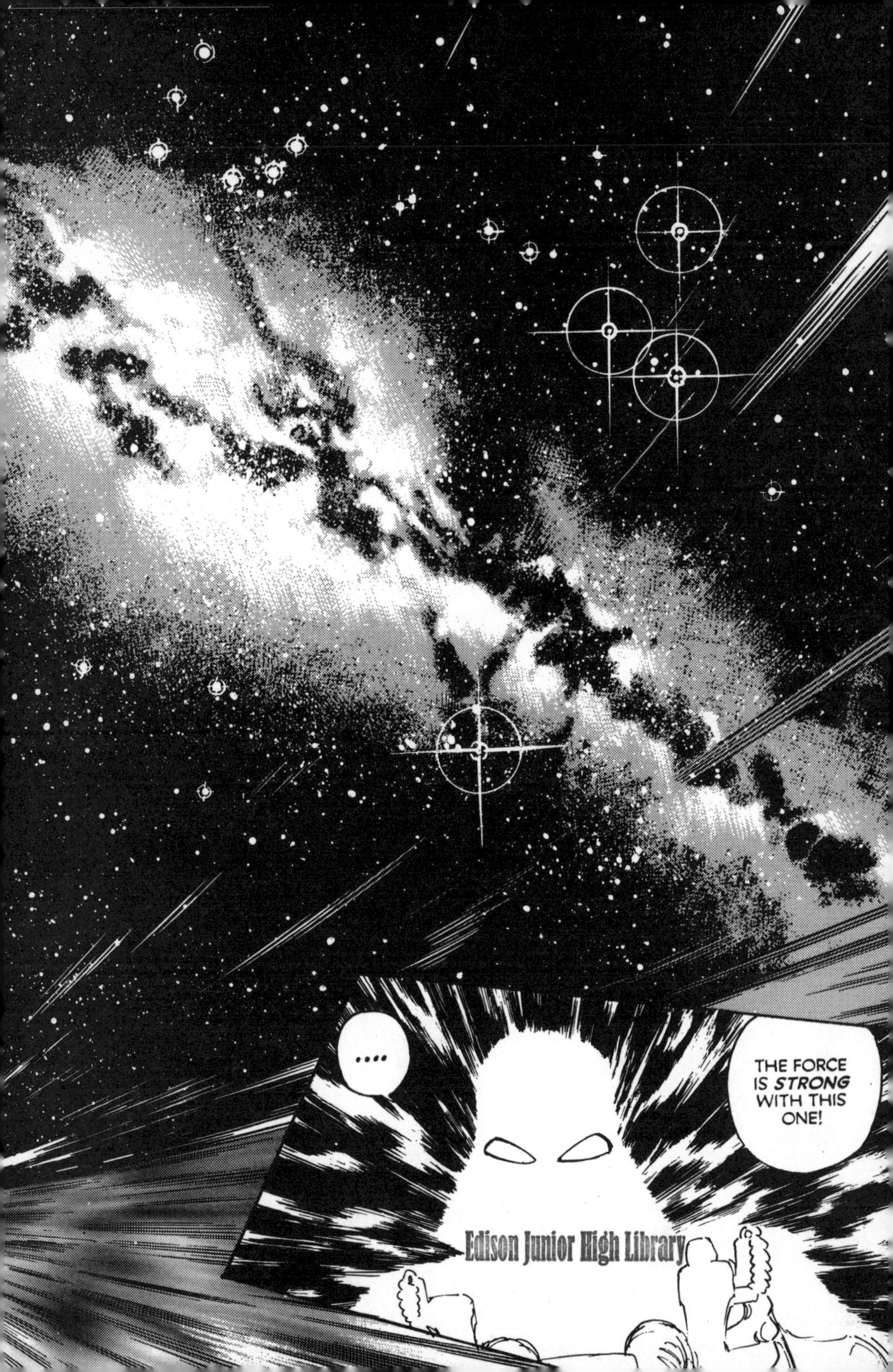
THE FORCE IS STRONG WITH THIS ONE!
....

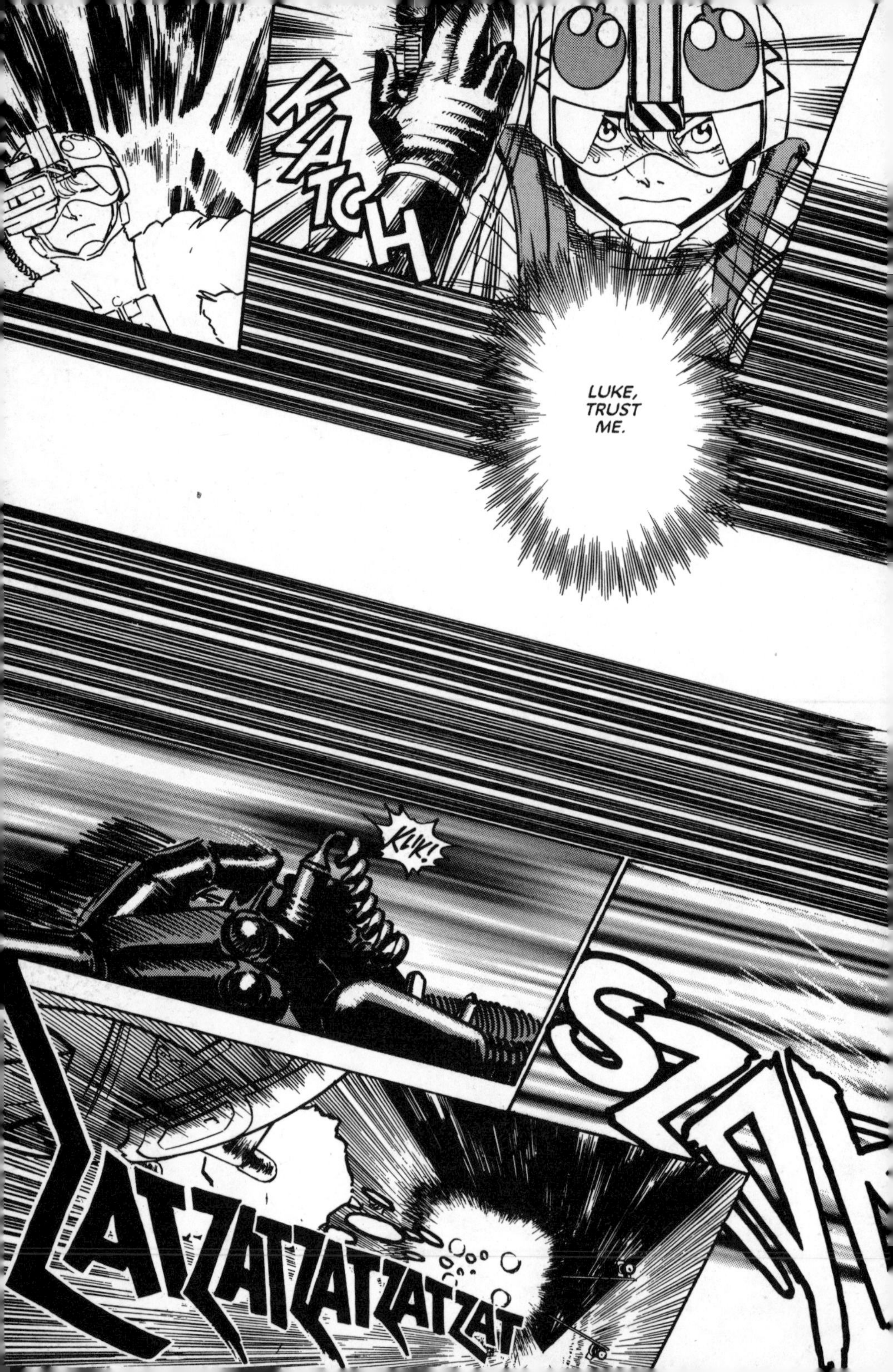
KLATCH
LUKE, TRUST ME.
KLIK!
SZAK
ZATZATZATZATZATZAT

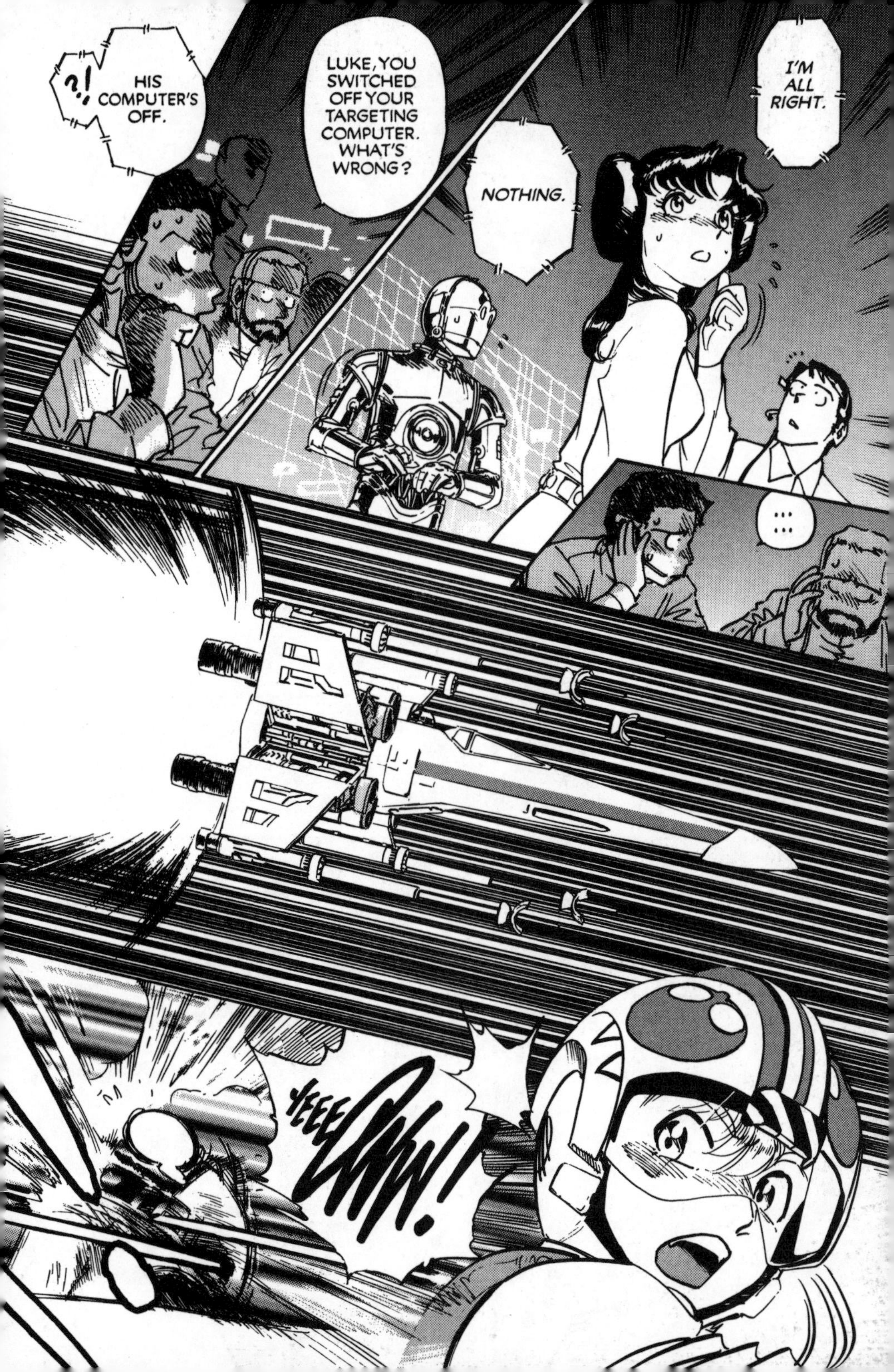
?!
HIS COMPUTER'S OFF.
LUKE, YOU SWITCHED OFF YOUR TARGETING COMPUTER. WHAT'S WRONG?
NOTHING.
I'M ALL RIGHT.
...
YEEEOWW!

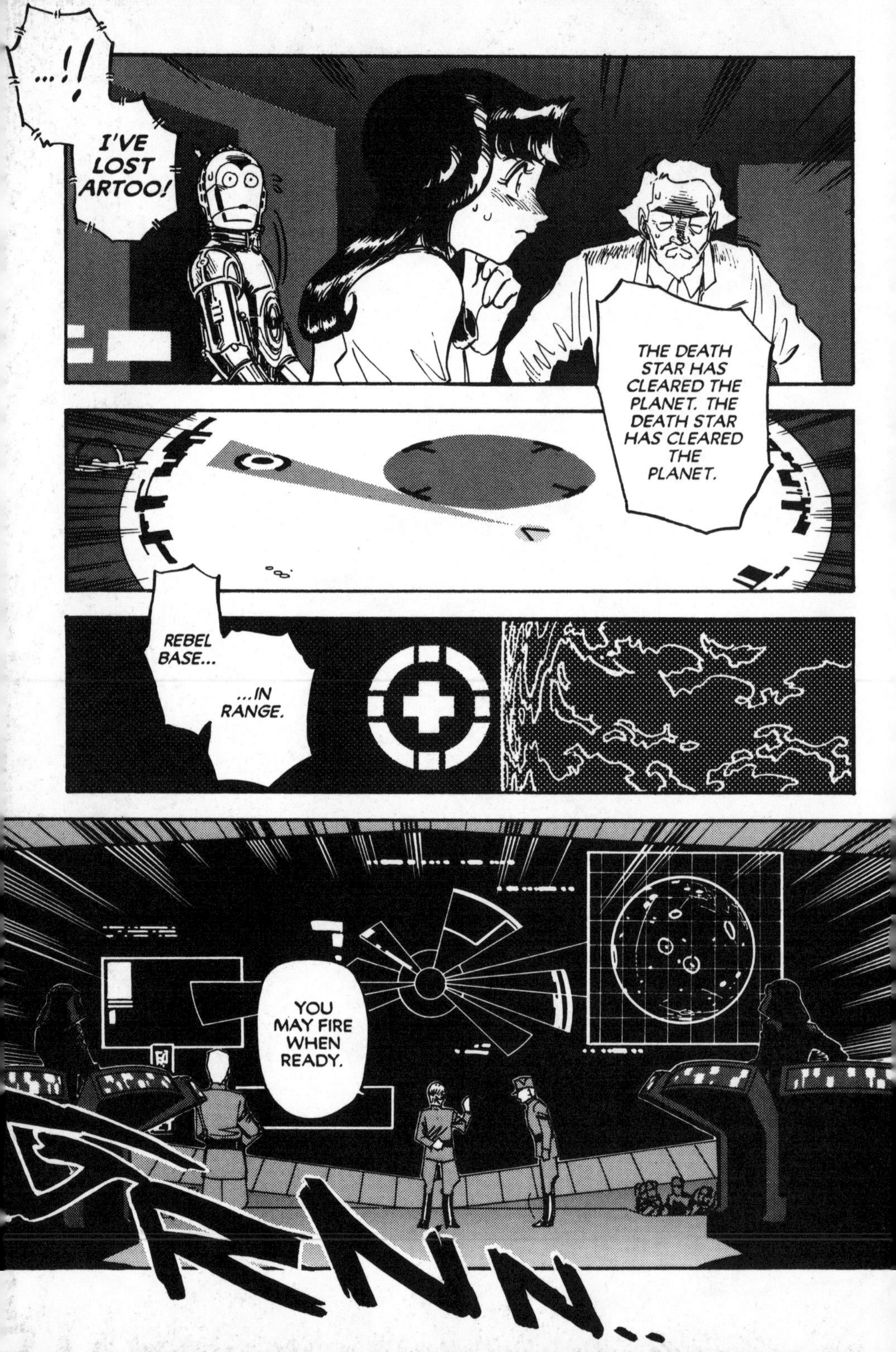
...!!
I'VE LOST ARTOO!
THE DEATH STAR HAS CLEARED THE PLANET. THE DEATH STAR HAS CLEARED THE PLANET.
REBEL BASE...
...IN RANGE.
YOU MAY FIRE WHEN READY.
ZRNN...

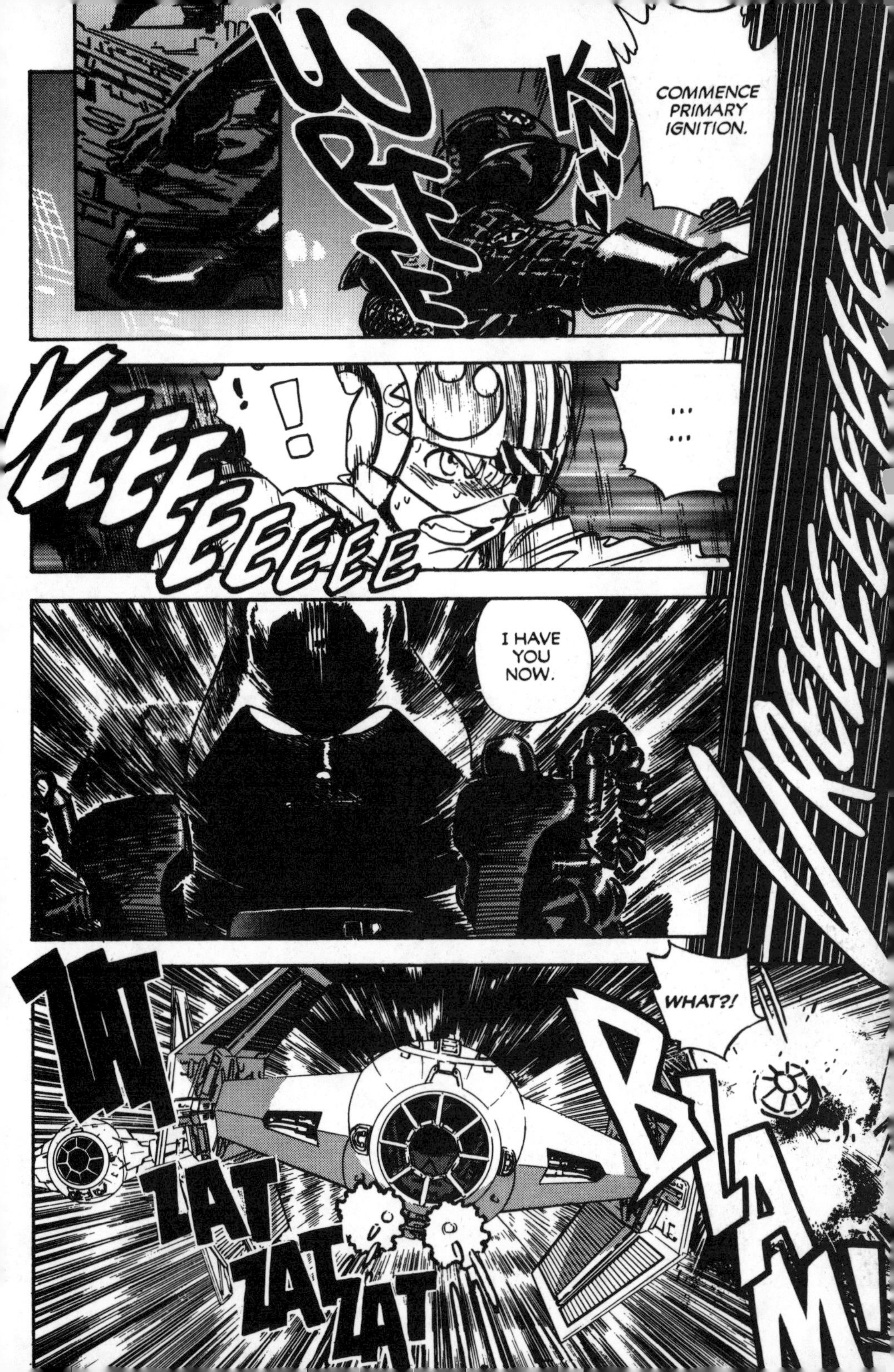
COMMENCE PRIMARY IGNITION.
!
!
...
...
I HAVE YOU NOW.
WHAT?!
BLAM!

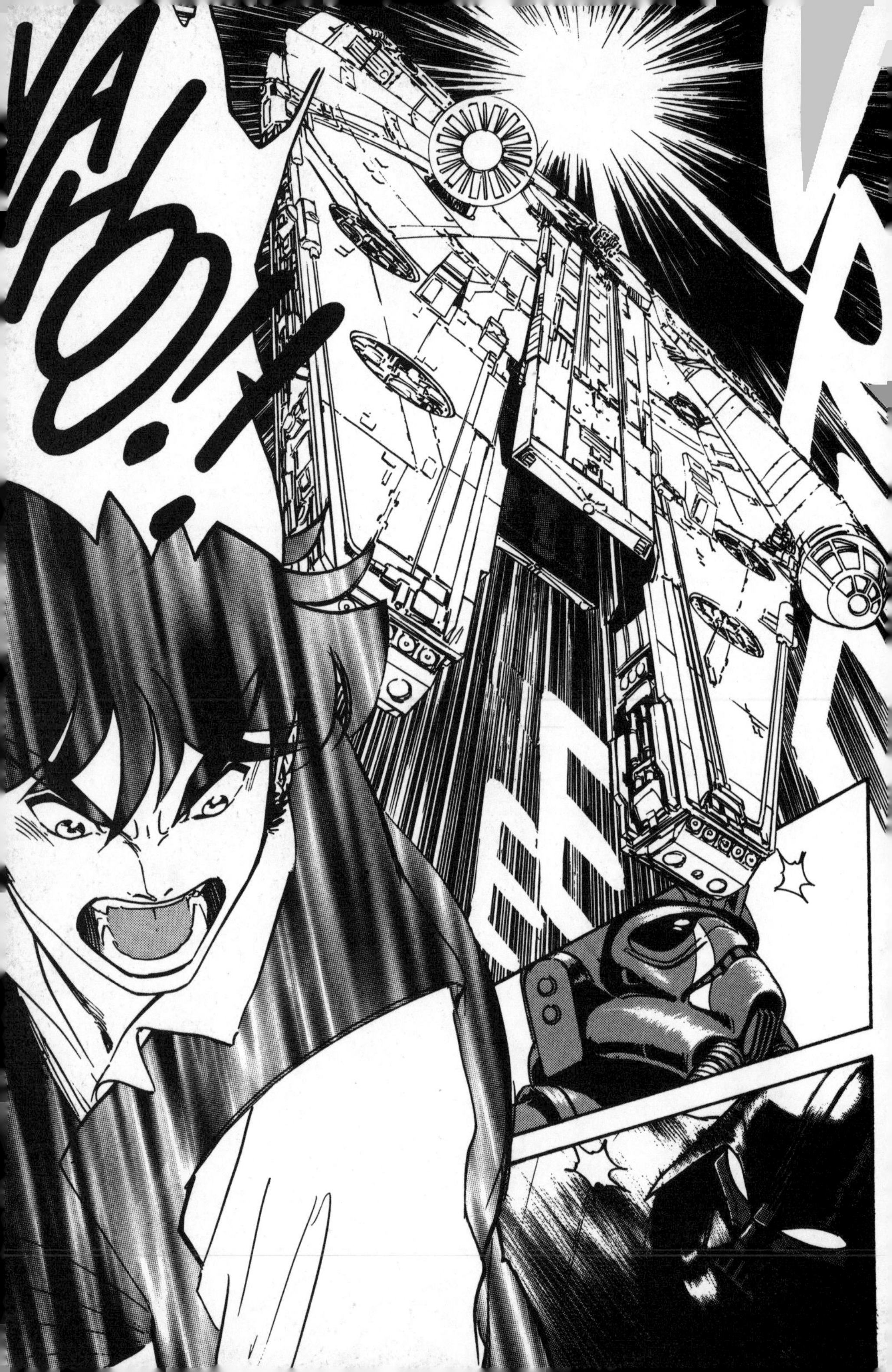
YAHOO!!

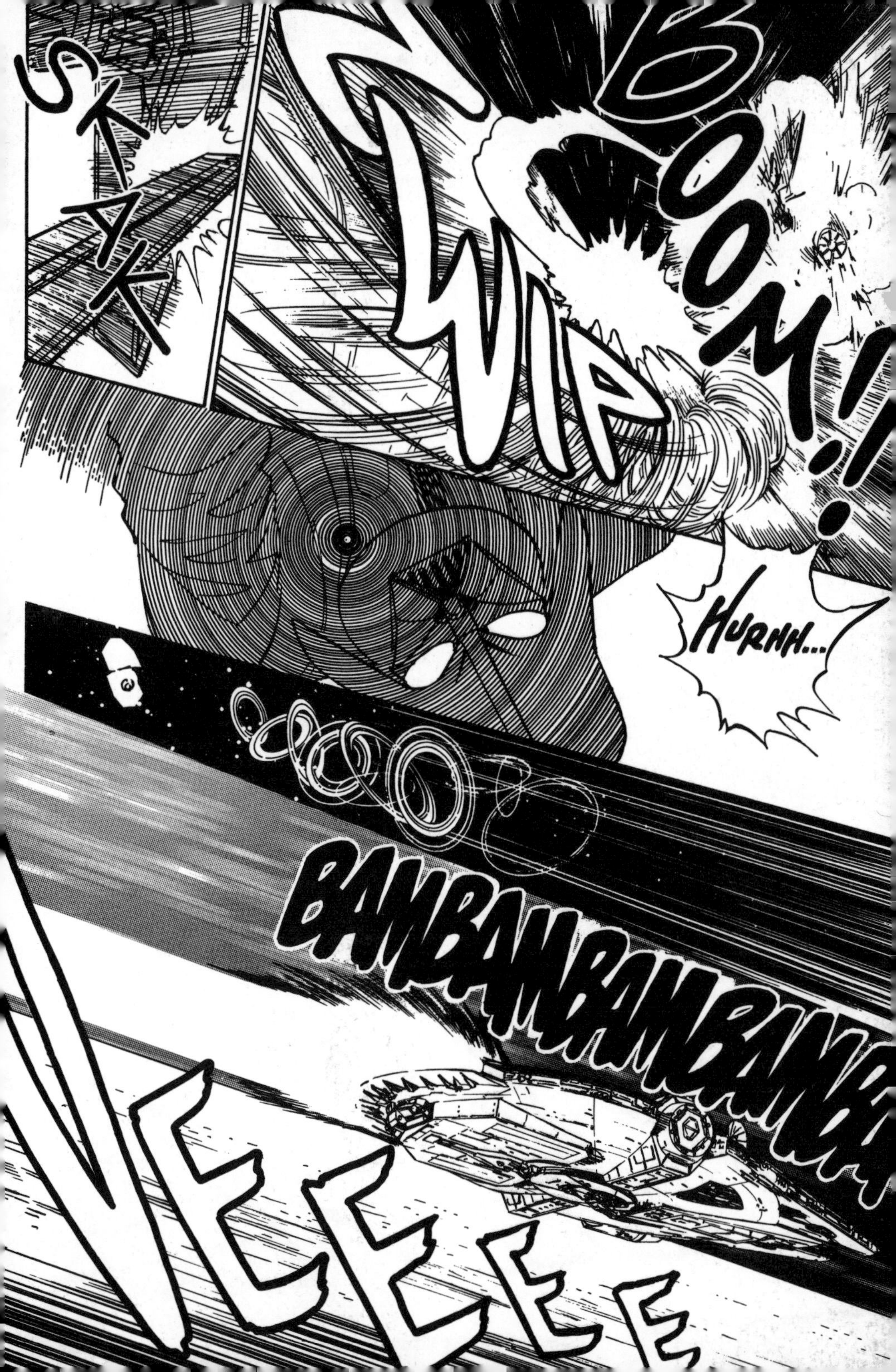
SKAK
ZWIP
BOOOM!!!
HURNH...
BANBANBANBANBAN
VEEEEE

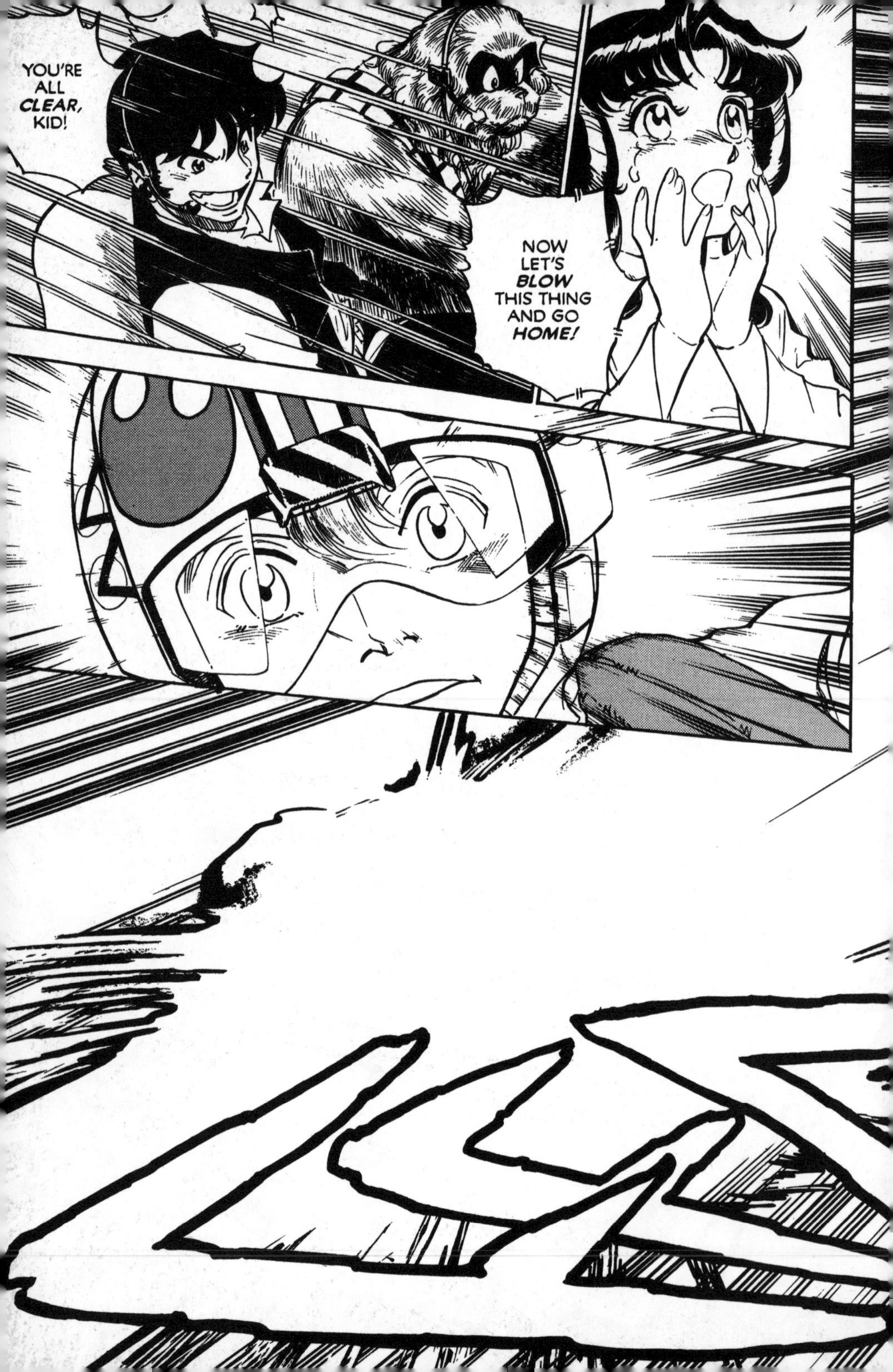
YOU'RE ALL *CLEAR,* KID!
NOW LET'S *BLOW* THIS THING AND GO *HOME!*

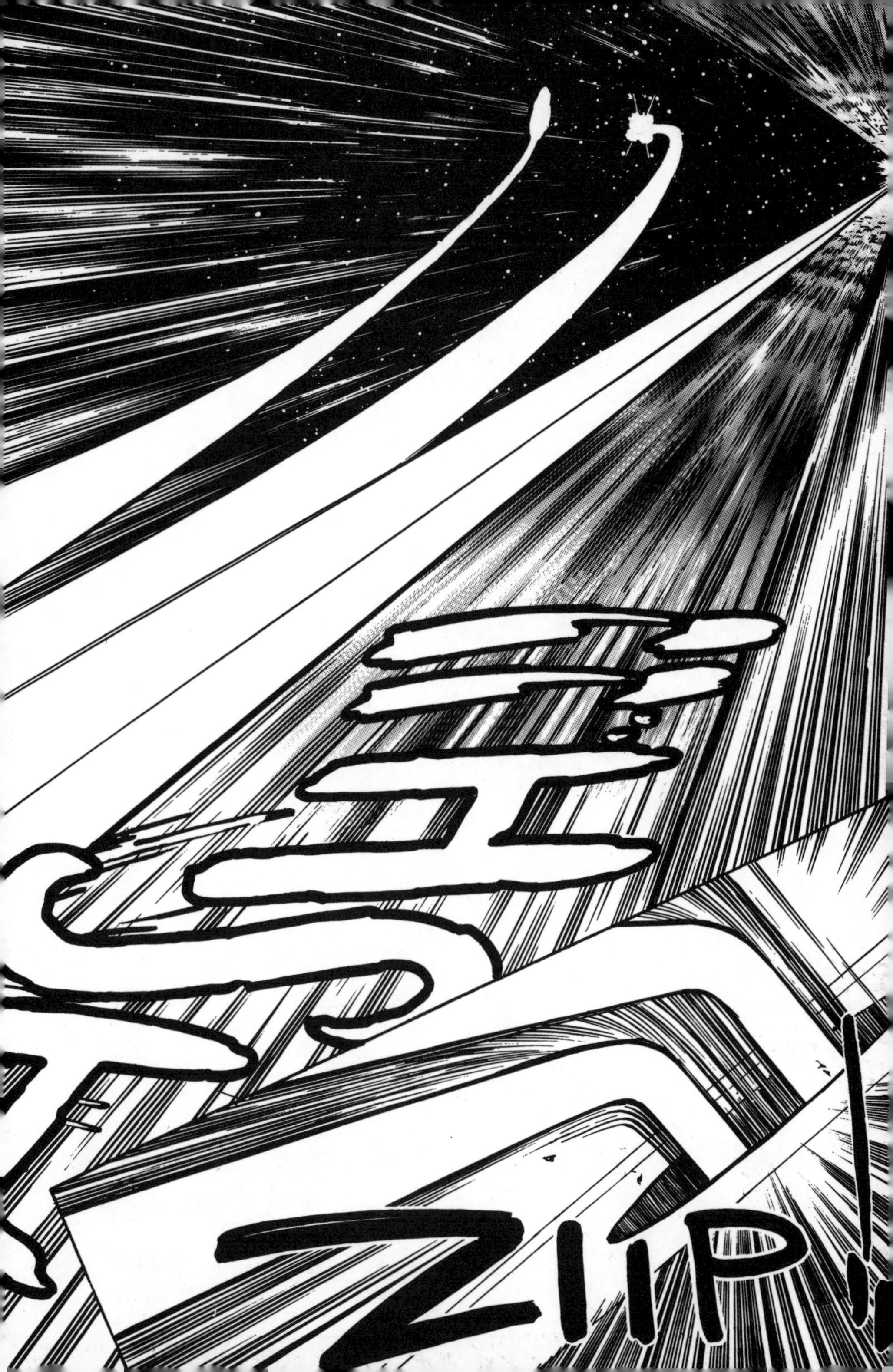
ZIP!!

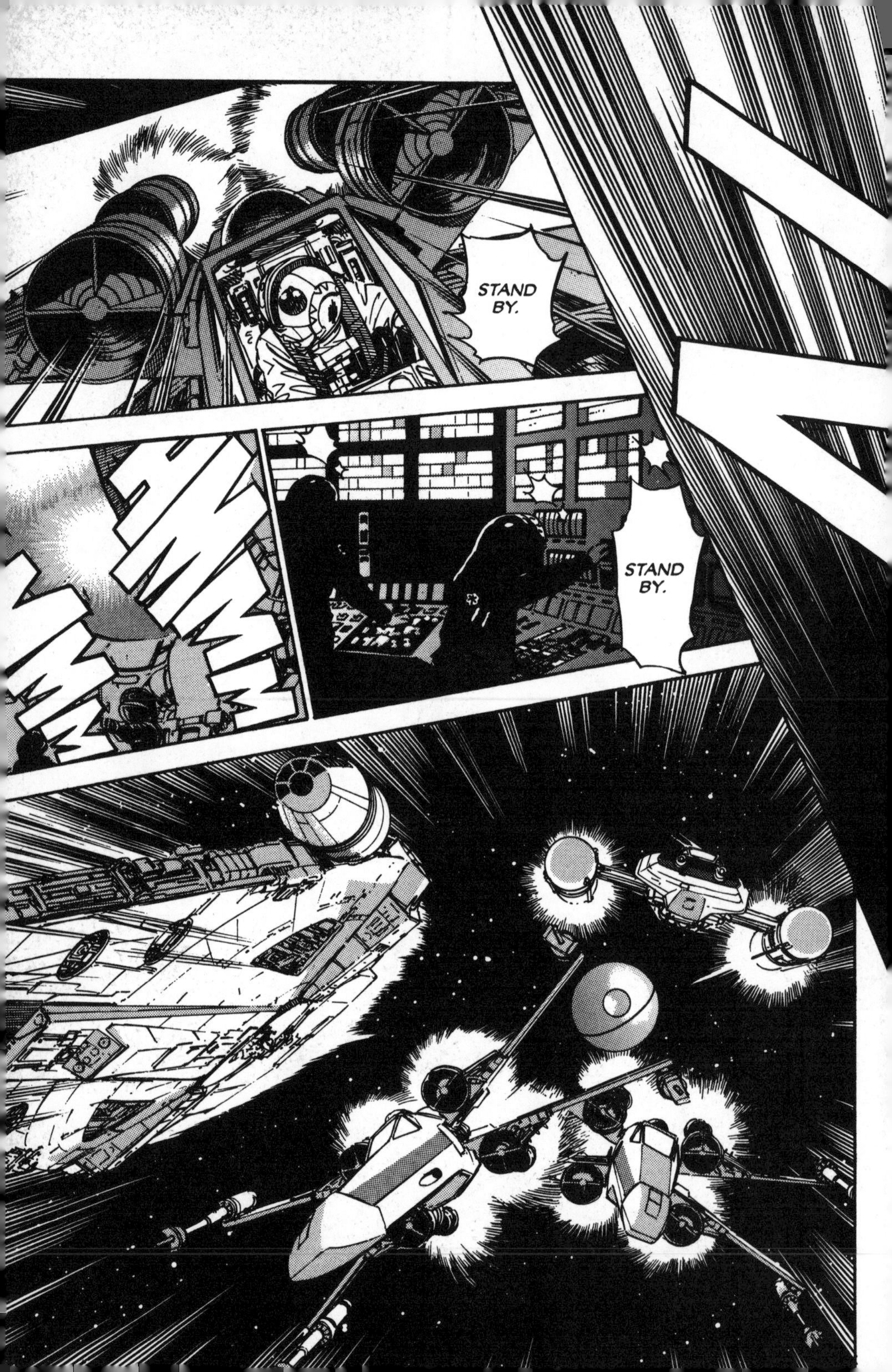
STAND BY.
STAND BY.

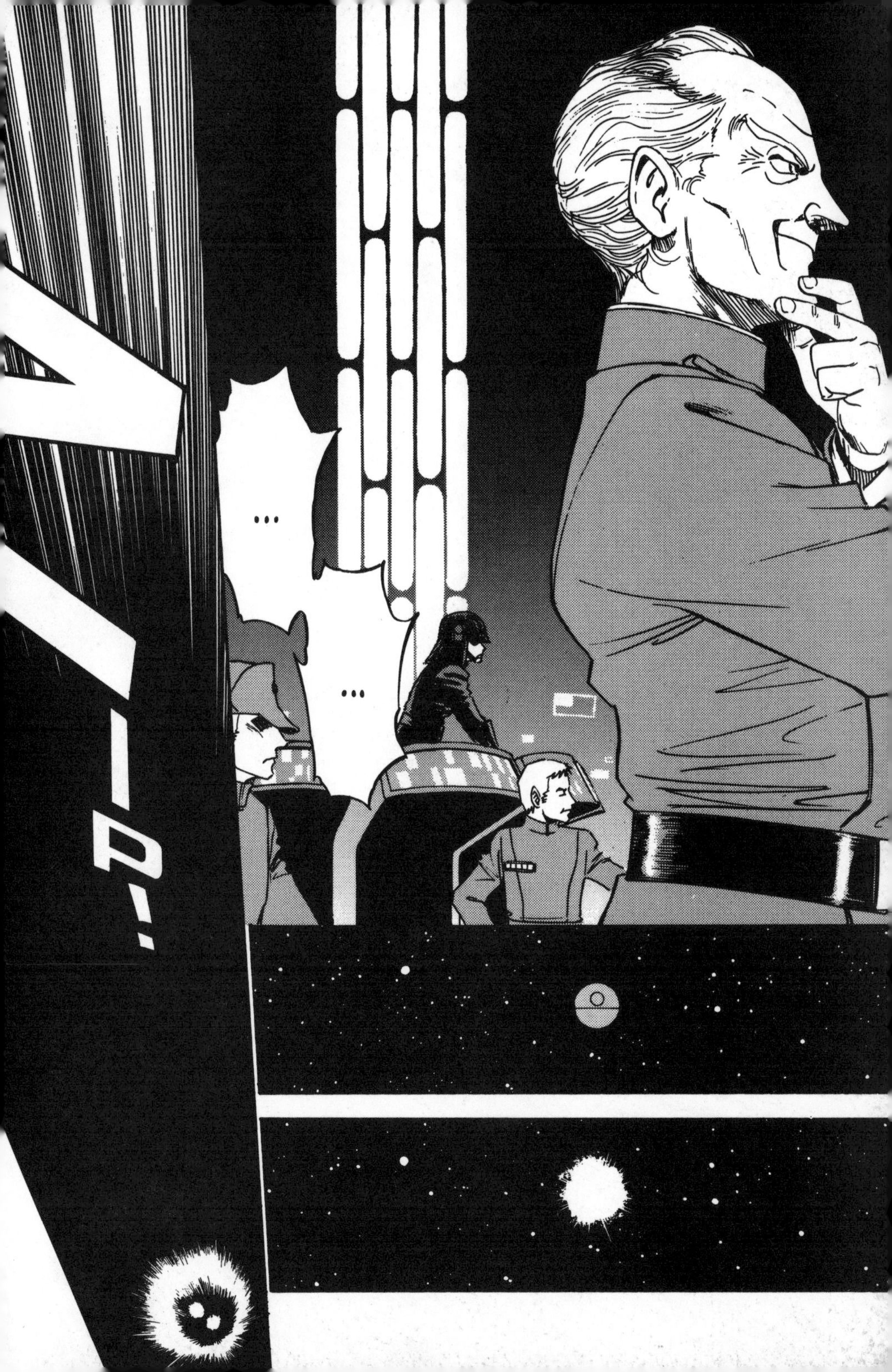
...
...

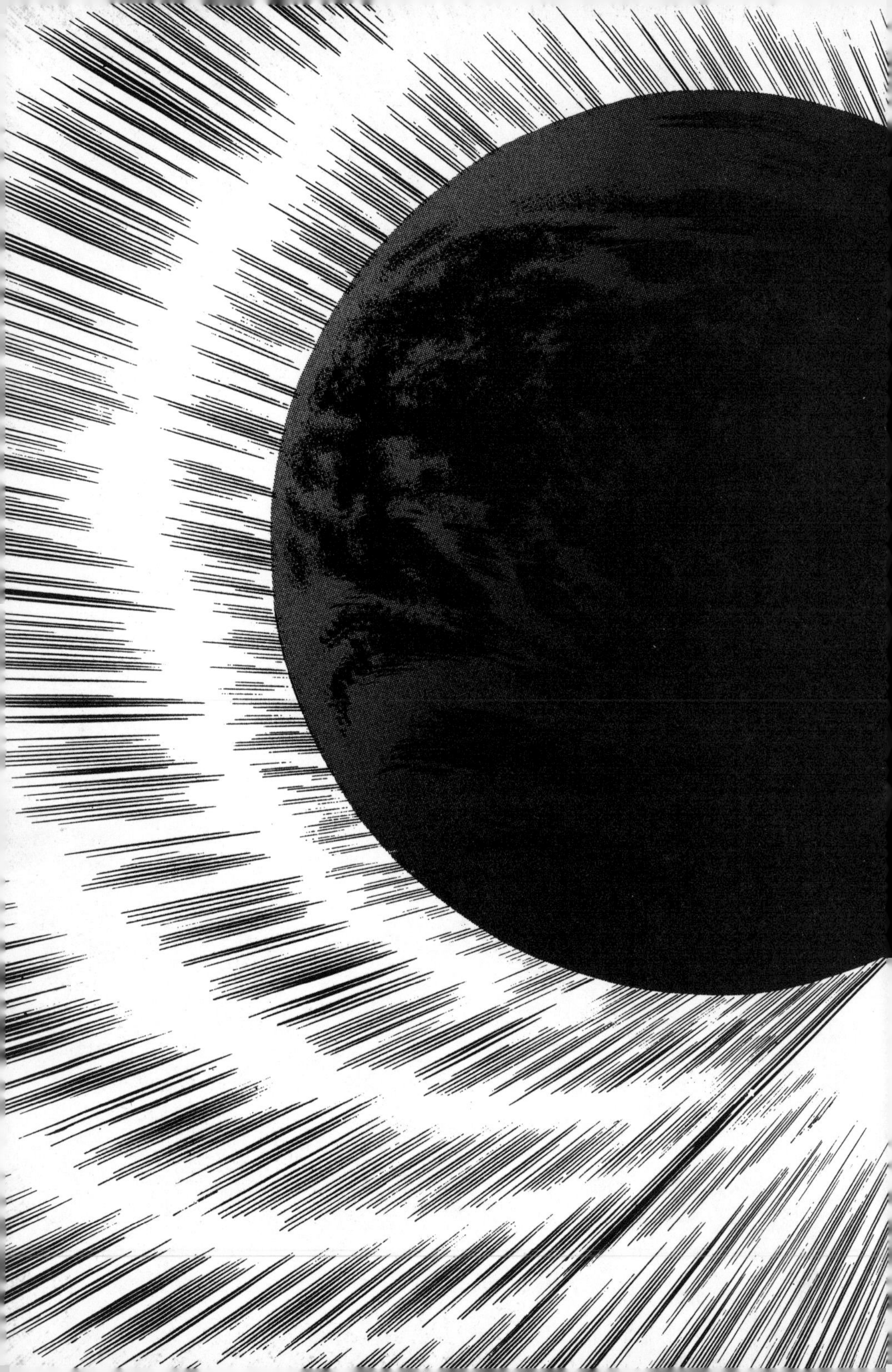

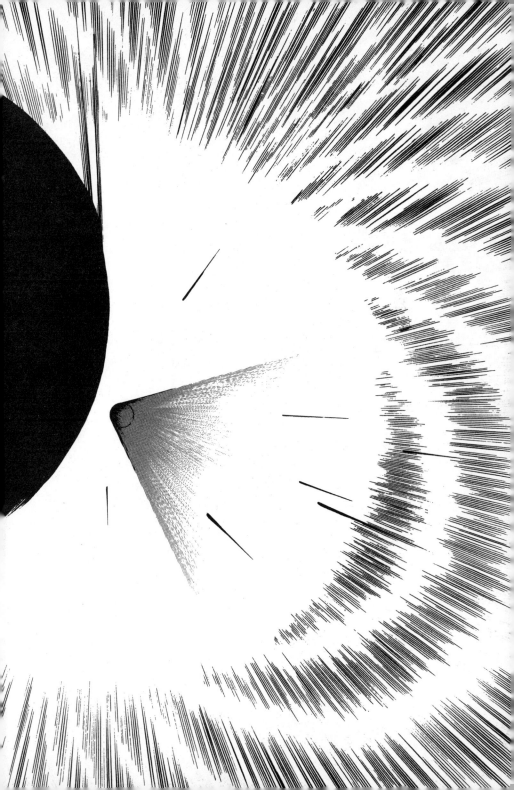

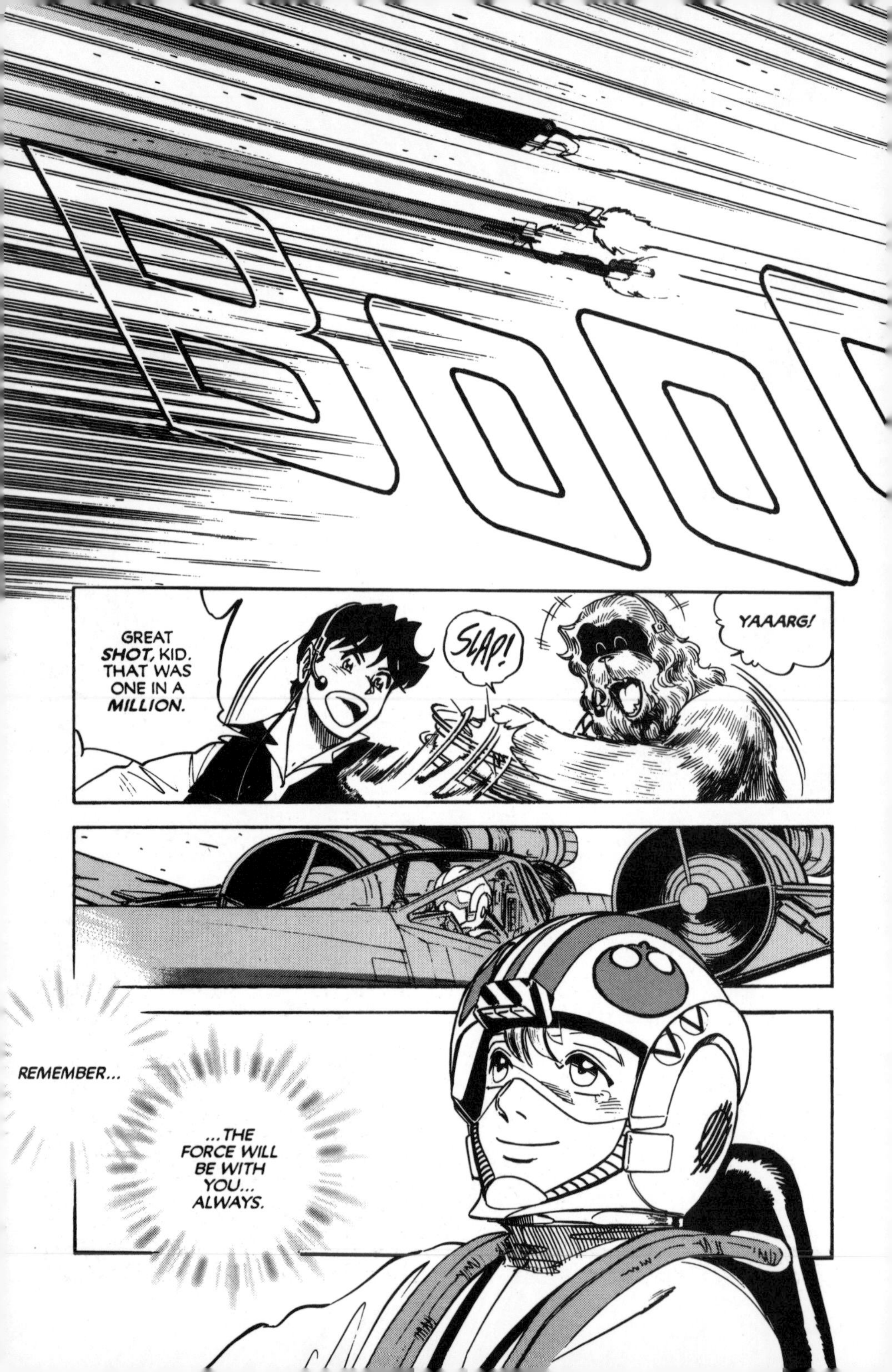
BOOO
GREAT SHOT, KID. THAT WAS ONE IN A MILLION.
SLAP!
YAAARG!
REMEMBER...
...THE FORCE WILL BE WITH YOU... ALWAYS.

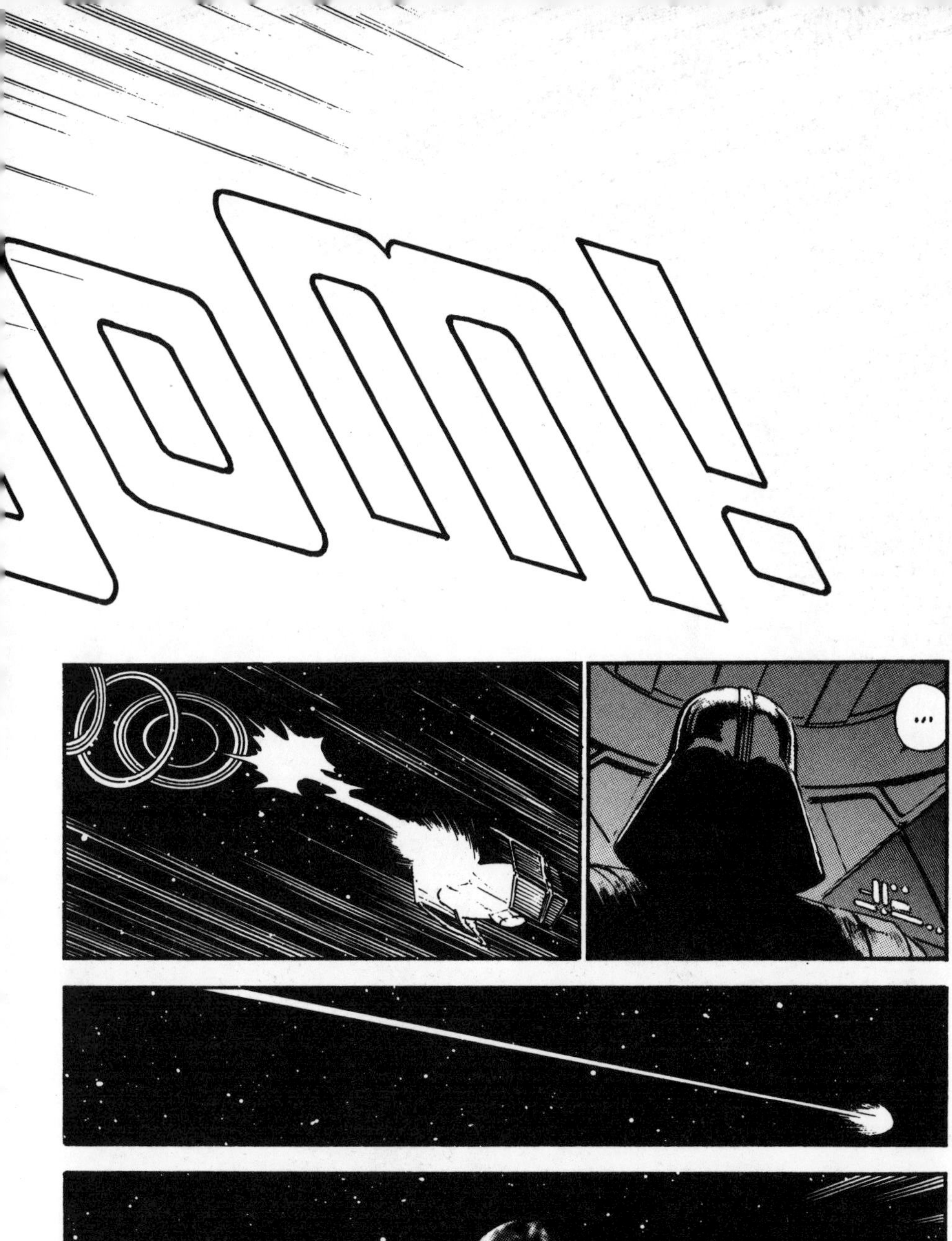
...

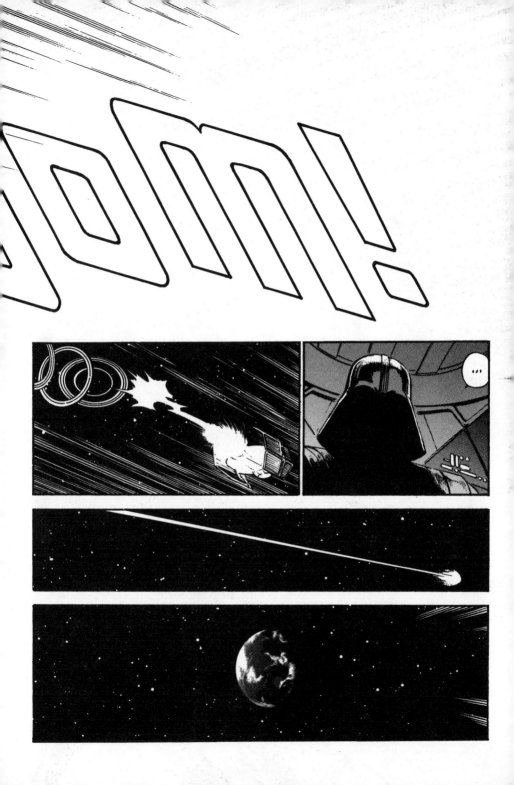

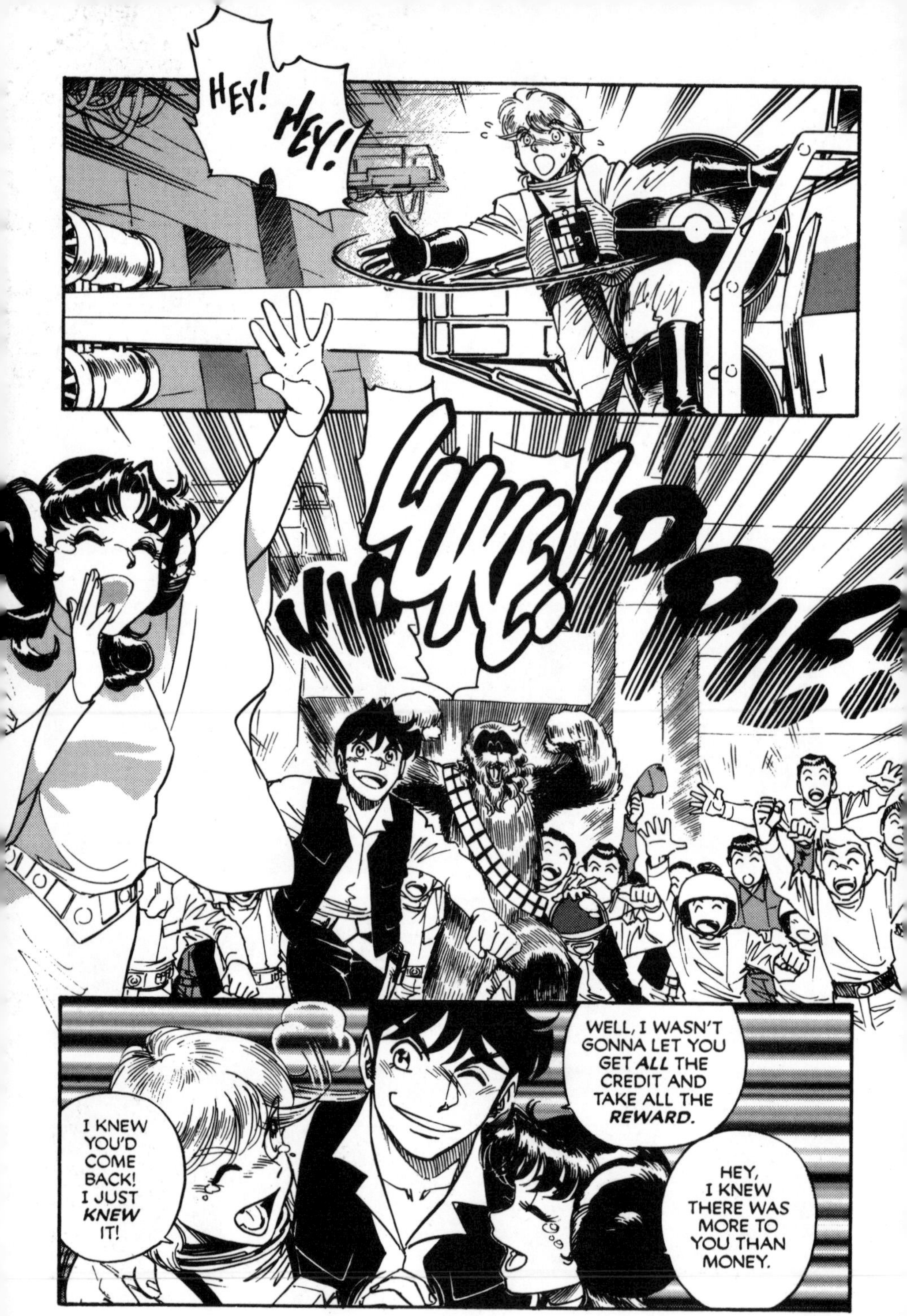
HEY!
HEY!
LUKE!
I KNEW YOU'D COME BACK! I JUST *KNEW* IT!
WELL, I WASN'T GONNA LET YOU GET *ALL* THE CREDIT AND TAKE ALL THE *REWARD.*
HEY, I KNEW THERE WAS MORE TO YOU THAN MONEY.

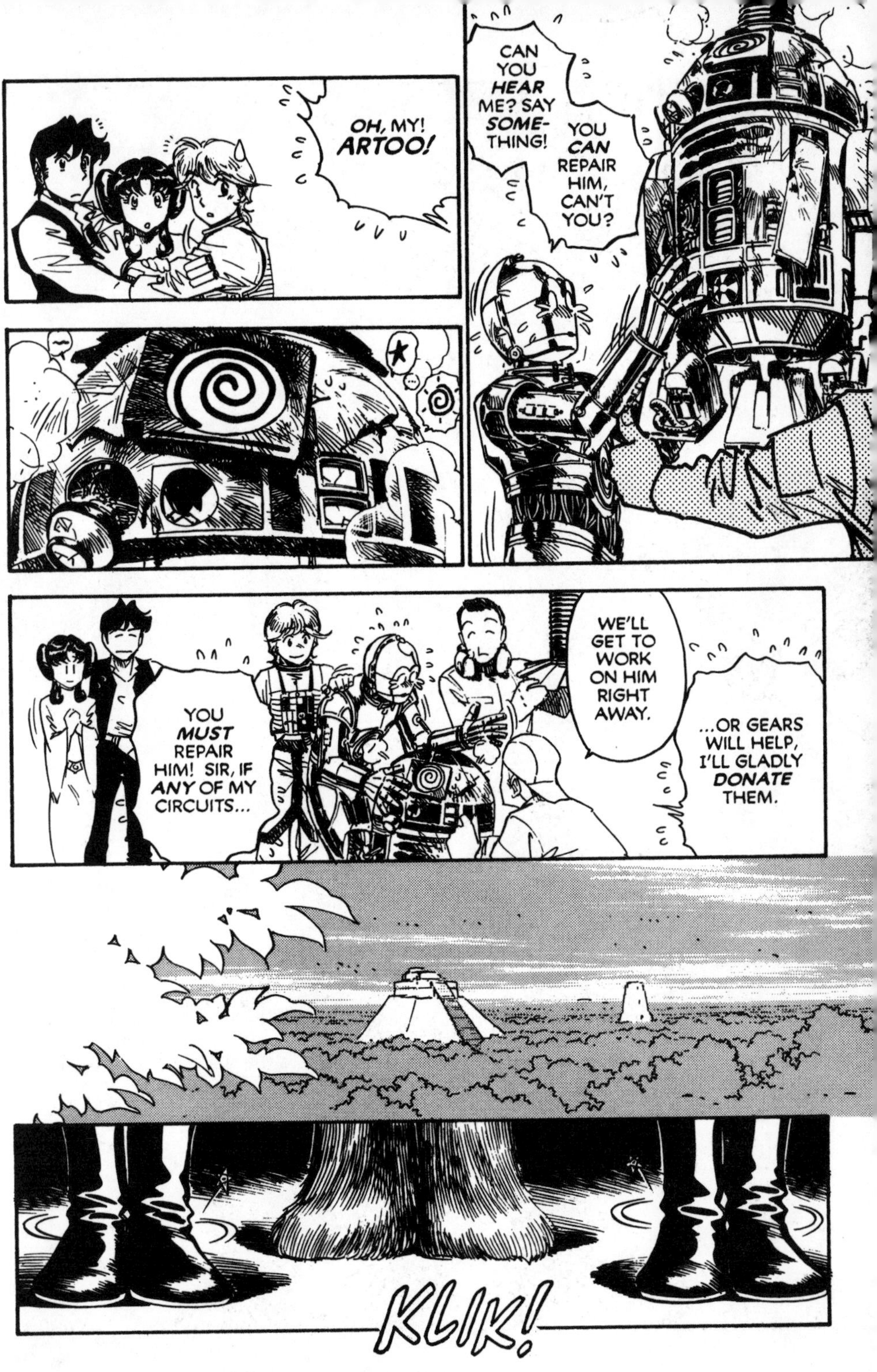
OH, MY! ARTOO!
CAN YOU HEAR ME? SAY SOME-THING!
YOU CAN REPAIR HIM, CAN'T YOU?
YOU MUST REPAIR HIM! SIR, IF ANY OF MY CIRCUITS...
WE'LL GET TO WORK ON HIM RIGHT AWAY.
...OR GEARS WILL HELP, I'LL GLADLY DONATE THEM.
KLIK!

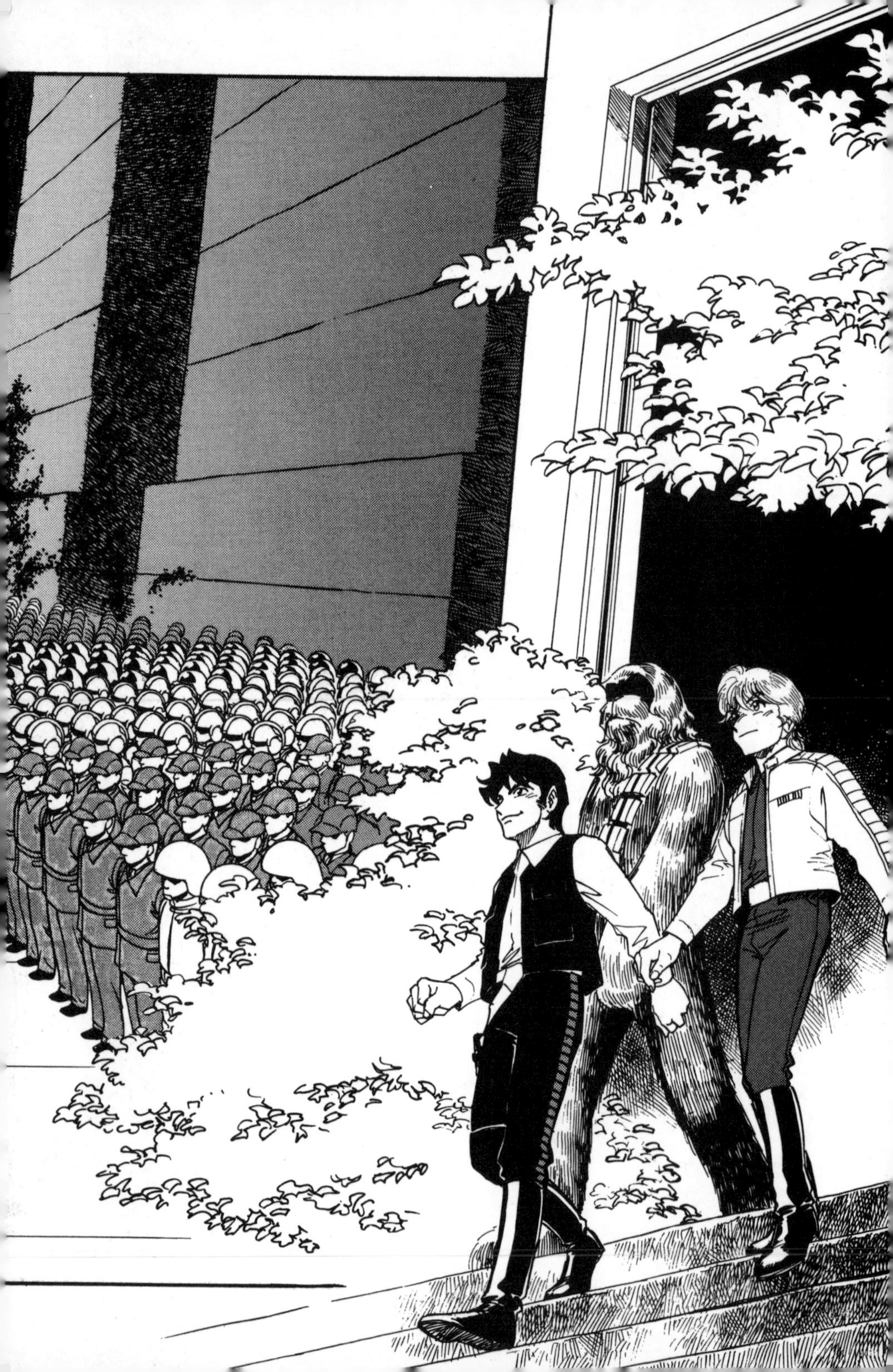

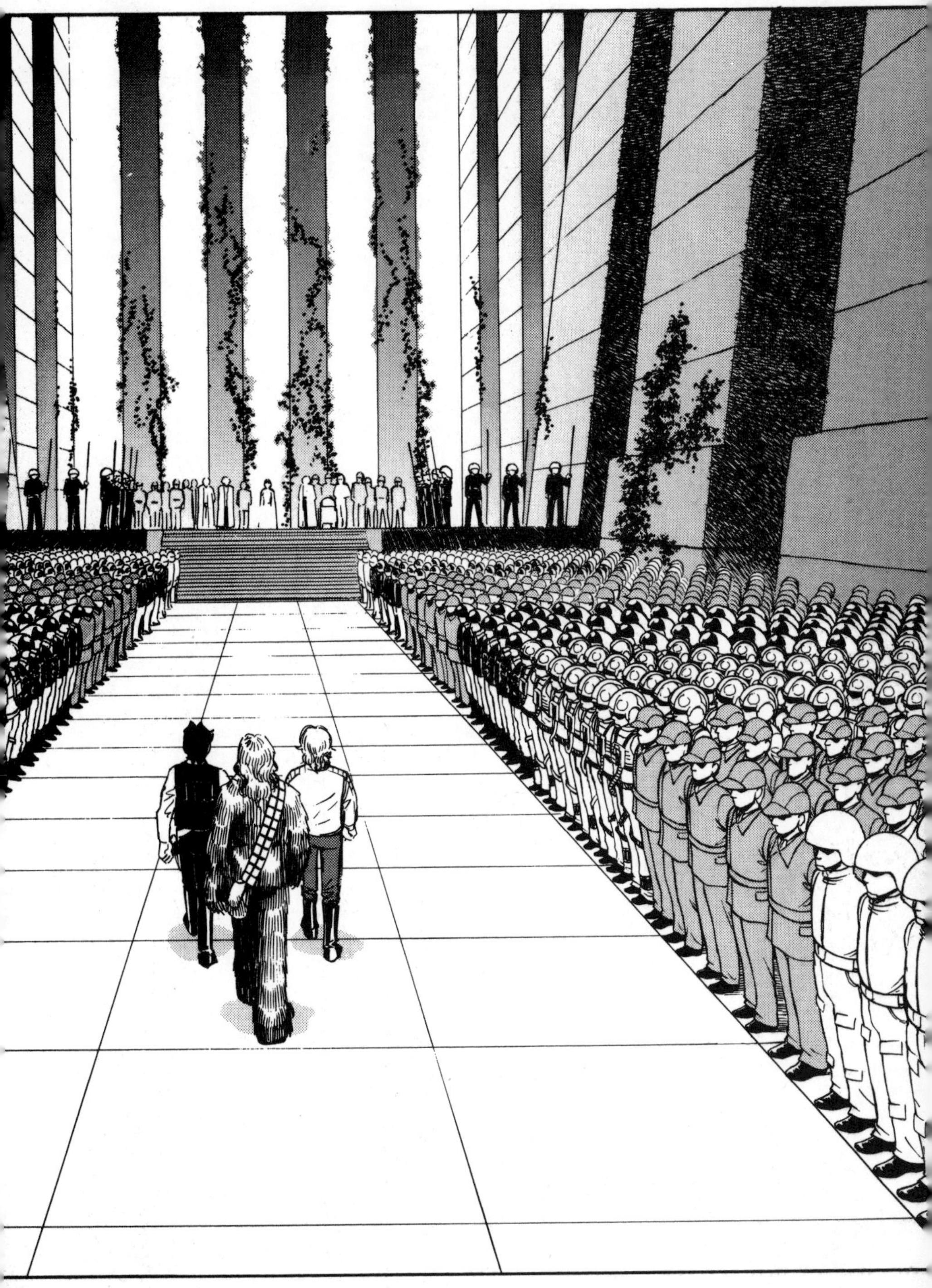

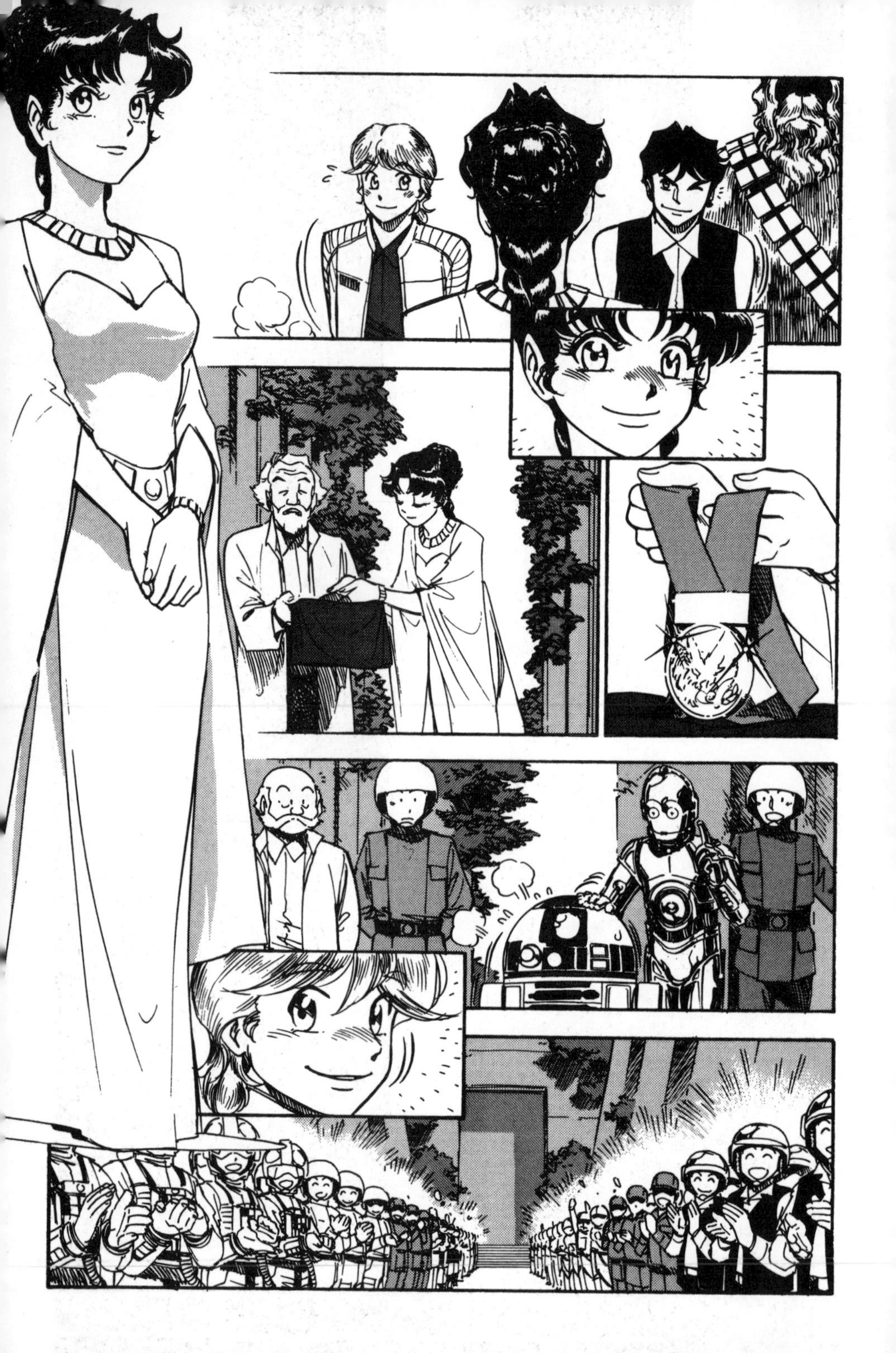

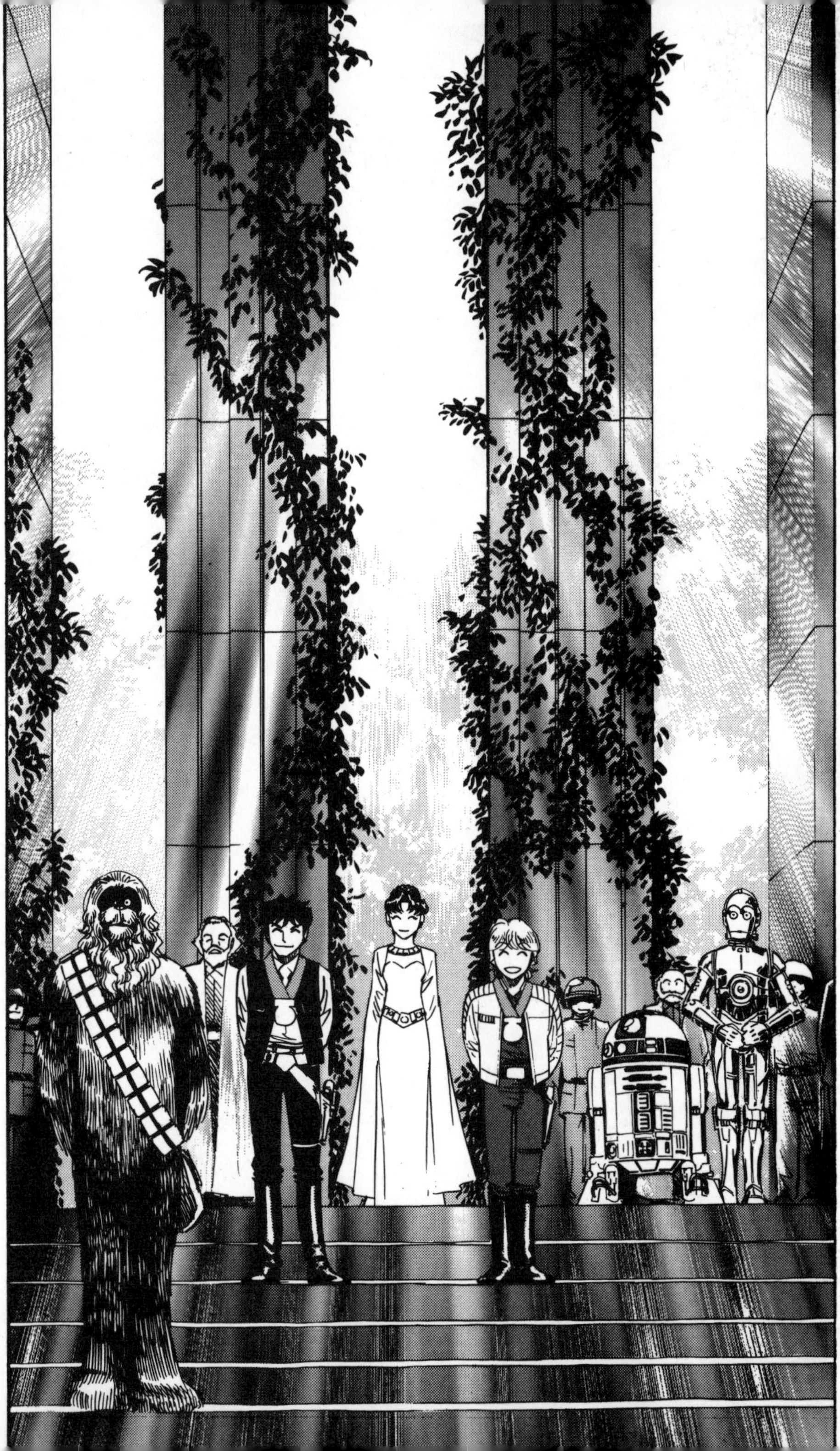

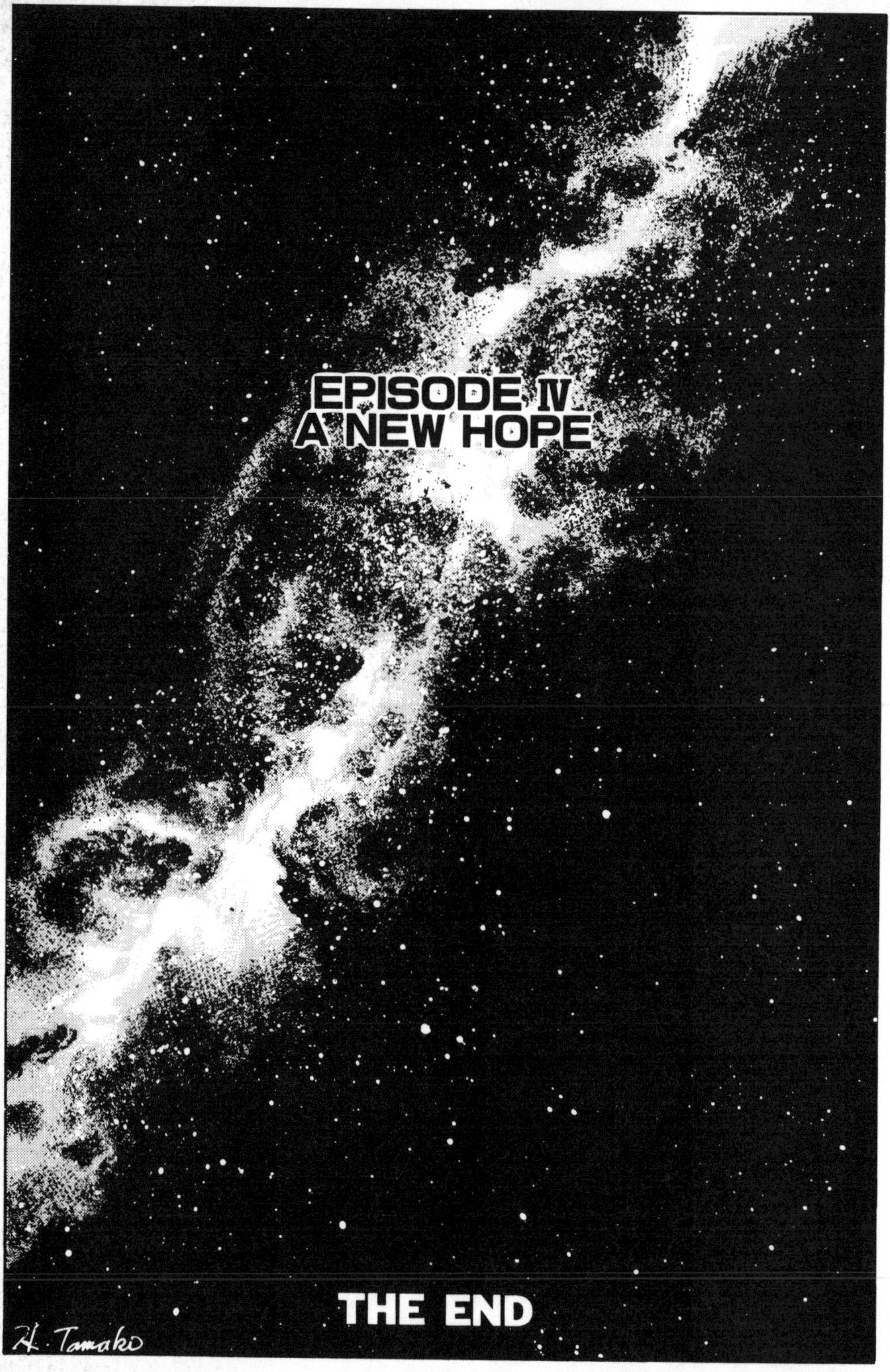
EPISODE IV
A NEW HOPE
THE END
H. Tamaki

スター・ウォーズ HISAO TAMAKI SKETCH GALLERY

The following is a sketch by artist Hisao Tamaki, done in preparation for his work on STAR WARS: A NEW HOPE — MANGA.

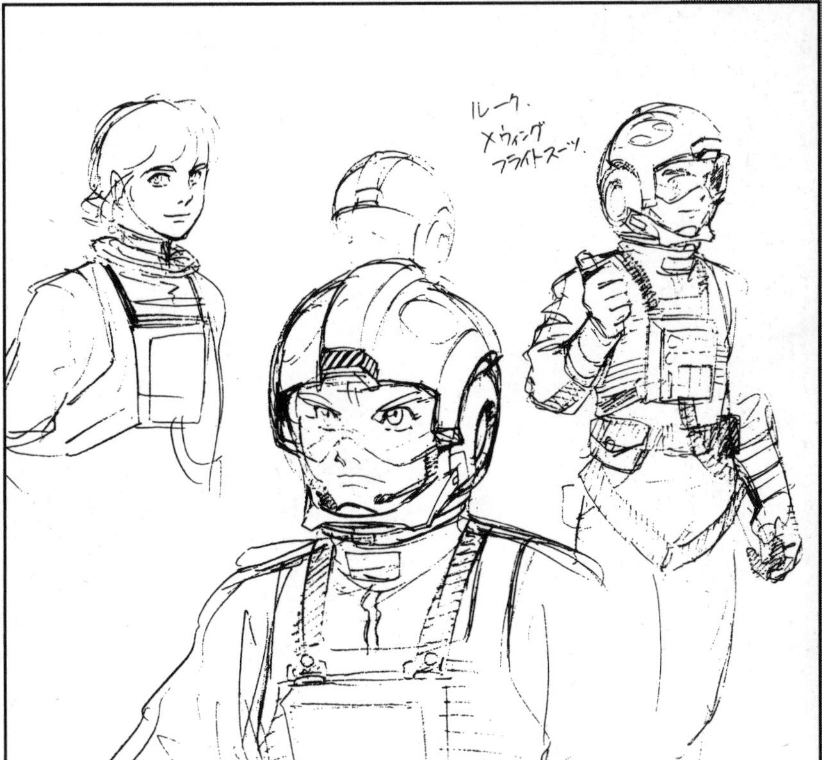
ルーク.
Xウィング
フライトスーツ.

LUKE SKYWALKER
IN X-WING PILOT GEAR

スター・ウォーズ
ADAM WARREN
SKETCH GALLERY

The following is a sketch by cover artist Adam Warren, done in preparation for the final cover of STAR WARS: A NEW HOPE — MANGA volume four.

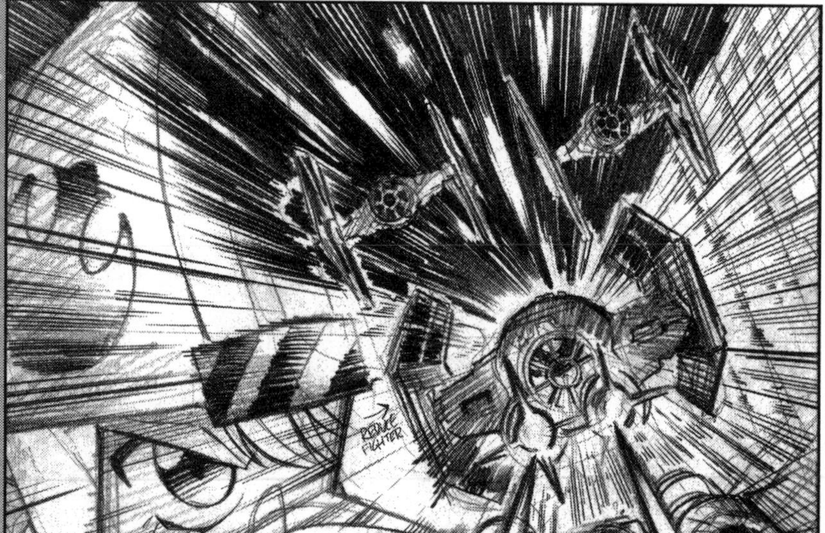
REDUCE
FIGHTER

ORIGINAL COVER SKETCH FOR STAR WARS MANGA VOLUME FOUR

ADAPTED FROM AN ORIGINAL SCRIPT BY GEORGE LUCAS

ILLUSTRATION BY HISAO TAMAKI

スター・ウォーズ 3
新たなる希望

LETTERING AND ART RETOUCH BY TOM ORZECHOWSKI

COVER ART BY ADAM WARREN

COVER COLORS BY JOSEPH WIGHT

SPECIAL THANKS TO ALLAN KAUSCH AND LUCY AUTREY WILSON AT LUCAS LICENSING

SPECIAL THANKS TO AMADOR CISNEROS AND MICHELLE STEWART

BOOK DESIGN BY CARY GRAZZINI

EDITED BY DAVID LAND

PUBLISHED BY MIKE RICHARDSON

 Published by Dark Horse Comics, Inc., 10956 SE Main Street, Milwaukie, OR 97222

ISBN: 1-56971-364-2   First edition: September 1998

10 9 8 7 6 5 4 3 2

PRINTED IN THE UNITED STATES OF AMERICA

スター・ウォーズ BACKLIST

A SAMPLING OF スター・ウォーズ GRAPHIC NOVELS FROM DARK HORSE COMICS

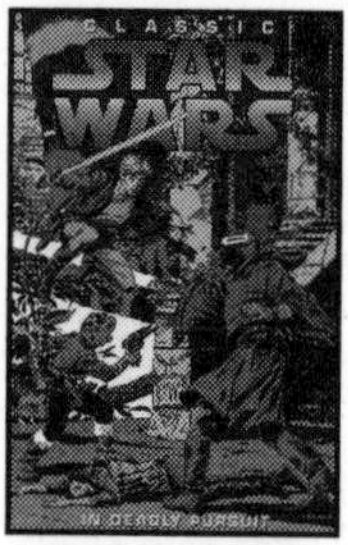
CLASSIC
STAR WARS
IN DEADLY PURSUIT

IN DEADLY PURSUIT
ISBN: 1-56971-109-7 $16.95

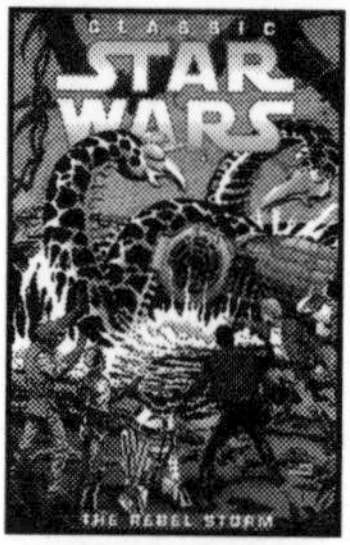
CLASSIC
STAR WARS
THE REBEL STORM

THE REBEL STORM
ISBN: 1-56971-106-2 $16.95

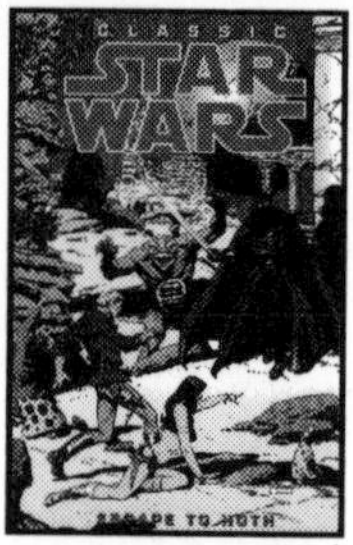
CLASSIC
STAR WARS
ESCAPE TO HOTH

ESCAPE TO HOTH
ISBN: 1-56971-093-7 $16.95

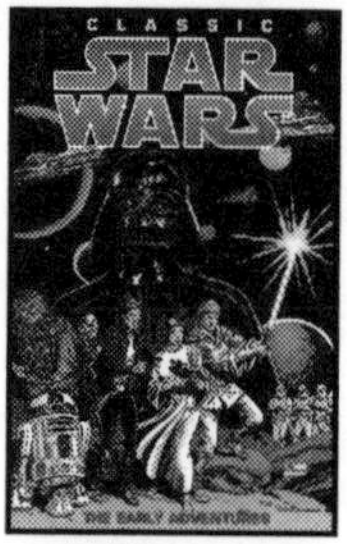
CLASSIC
STAR WARS

THE EARLY ADVENTURES
ISBN: 1-56971-178-X $19.95

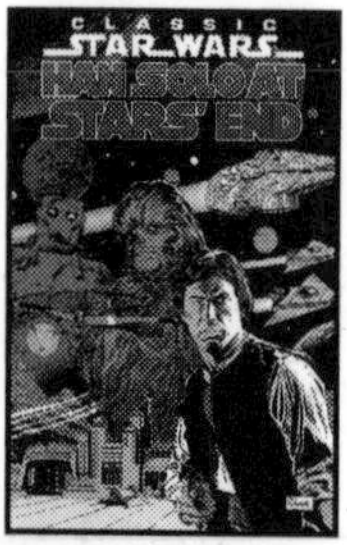
CLASSIC
STAR WARS
HAN SOLO AT STARS' END

HAN SOLO AT STARS' END
ISBN: 1-56971-254-9 $6.95

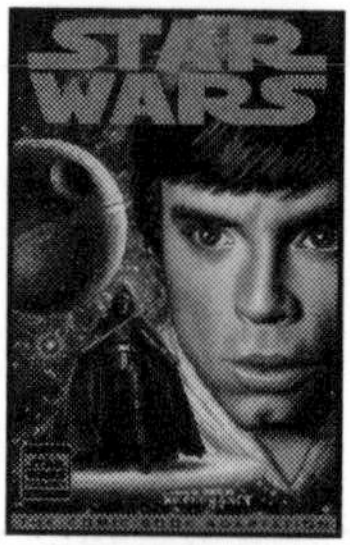
STAR WARS

A NEW HOPE
ISBN: 1-56971-213-1 $9.95

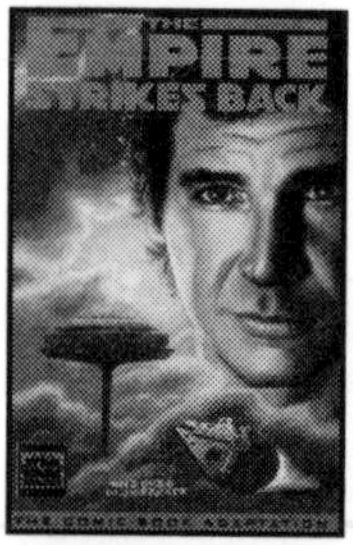
THE EMPIRE STRIKES BACK
THE COMIC BOOK ADAPTATION

THE EMPIRE STRIKES BACK
ISBN: 1-56971-234-4 $9.95

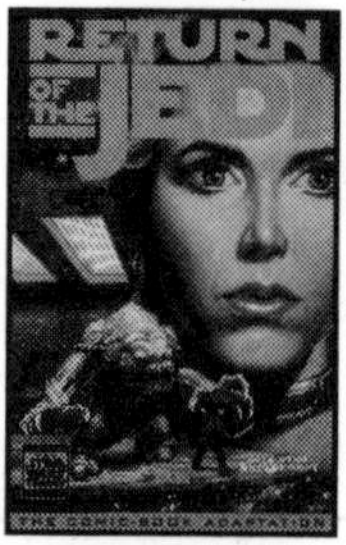
RETURN OF THE JEDI
THE COMIC BOOK ADAPTATION

RETURN OF THE JEDI
ISBN: 1-56971-235-2 $9.95

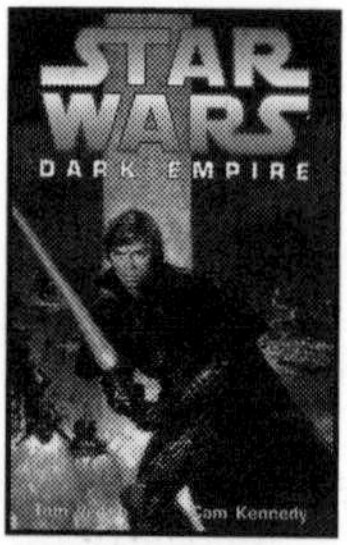
STAR WARS
DARK EMPIRE
Cam Kennedy

DARK EMPIRE
ISBN: 1-56971-073-2 $17.95

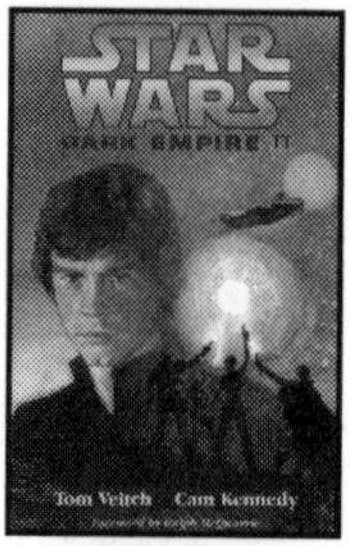
STAR WARS
DARK EMPIRE II
Tom Veitch Cam Kennedy

DARK EMPIRE II
ISBN: 1-56971-119-4 $17.95

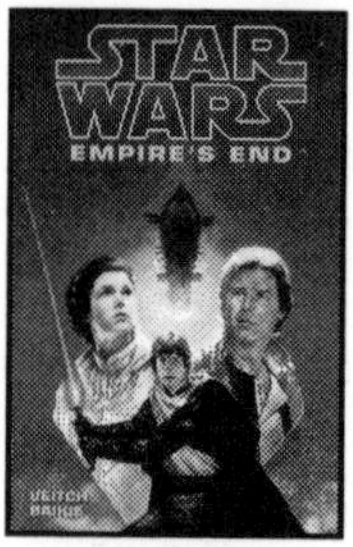
STAR WARS
EMPIRE'S END
VEITCH
BAIKIE

EMPIRE'S END
ISBN: 1-56971-306-5 $5.95

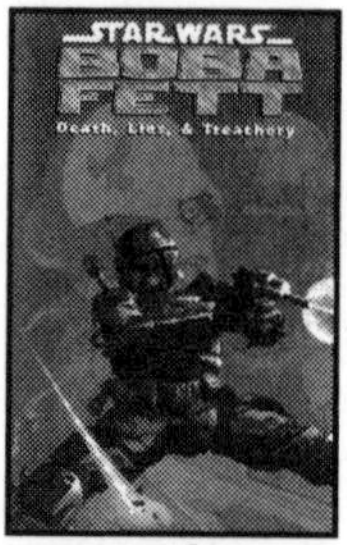
STAR WARS
BOBA FETT
Death, Lies, & Treachery

DEATH, LIES, & TREACHERY
ISBN: 1-56971-311-1 $12.95

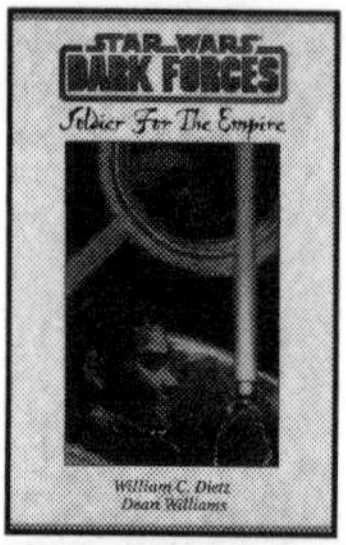
STAR WARS
DARK FORCES
Soldier For The Empire
William C. Dietz
Dean Williams

SOLDIER FOR THE EMPIRE HC
ISBN: 1-56971-155-0 $24.95

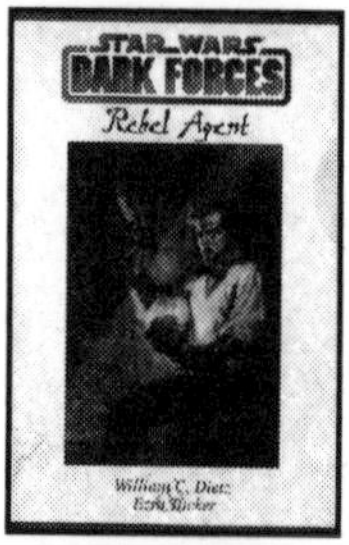
STAR WARS
DARK FORCES
Rebel Agent
William C. Dietz
Ezra Tucker

REBEL AGENT HC
ISBN: 1-56971-156-9 $24.95

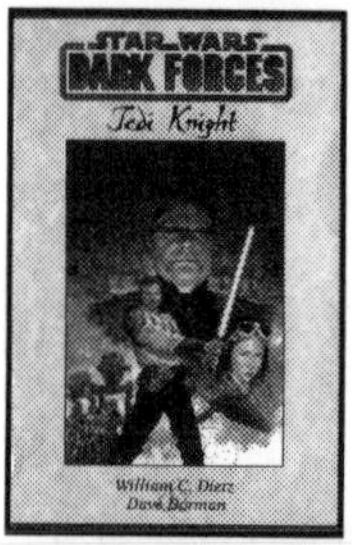
STAR WARS
DARK FORCES
Jedi Knight
William C. Dietz
Dave Dorman

JEDI KNIGHT HC
1-56971-157-7 $24.95

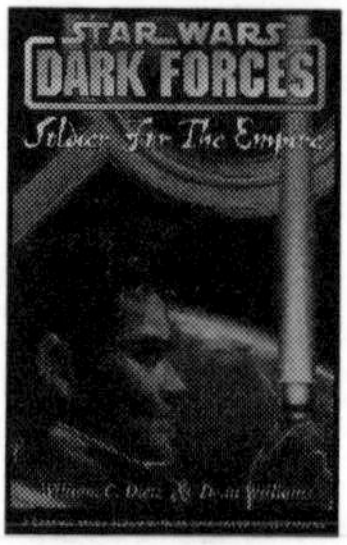
STAR WARS
DARK FORCES
Soldier For The Empire
William C. Dietz & Dean Williams

SOLDIER FOR THE EMPIRE
1-56971-348-0 $14.95

漫画 BACKLIST

A SAMPLING OF 漫画 GRAPHIC NOVELS FROM DARK HORSE COMICS

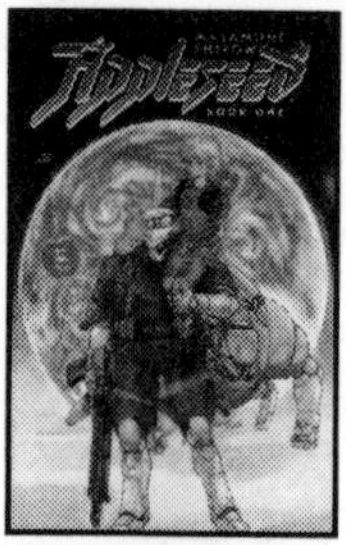

BOOK ONE
ISBN: 1-56971-070-8 $14.95

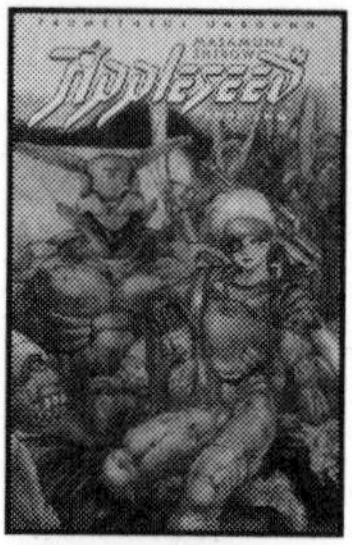

BOOK TWO
ISBN: 1-56971-071-6 $14.95

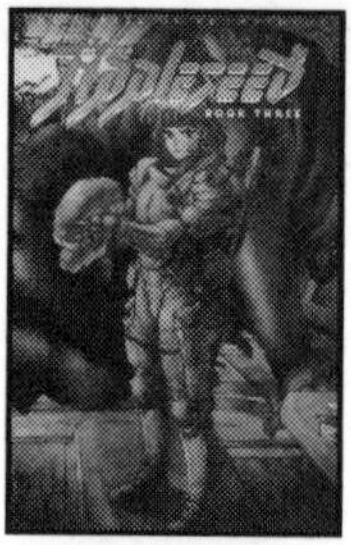
BOOK THREE

BOOK THREE
ISBN: 1-56971-072-4 $14.95

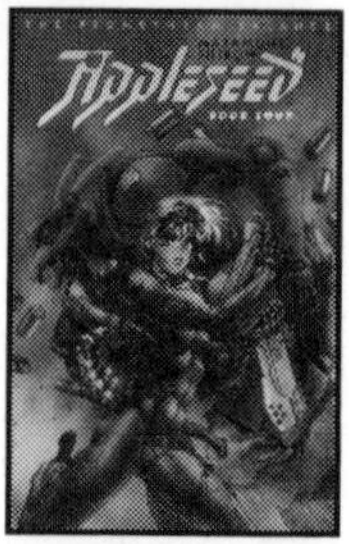

BOOK FOUR
ISBN: 1-56971-074-0 $14.95

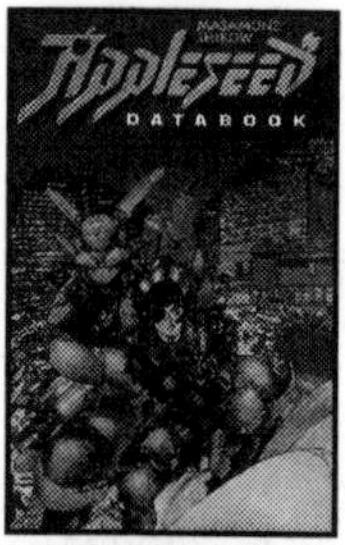
DATABOOK

DATABOOK
ISBN: 1-56971-103-8 $12.95

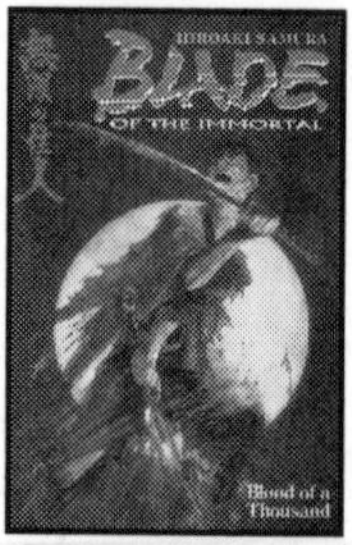
HIROAKI SAMURA
BLADE
OF THE IMMORTAL
Blood of a Thousand

BLOOD OF A THOUSAND
ISBN: 1-56971-239-5 $14.95

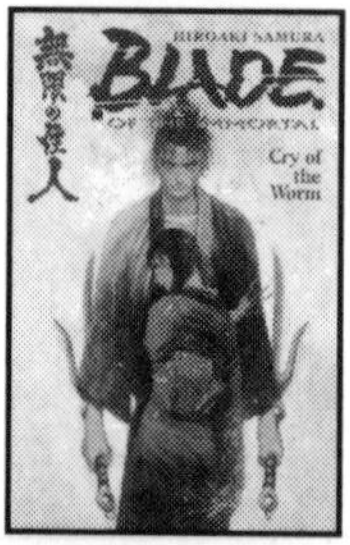
HIROAKI SAMURA
BLADE
Cry of the Worm

CRY OF THE WORM
ISBN: 1-56971-300-6 $12.95

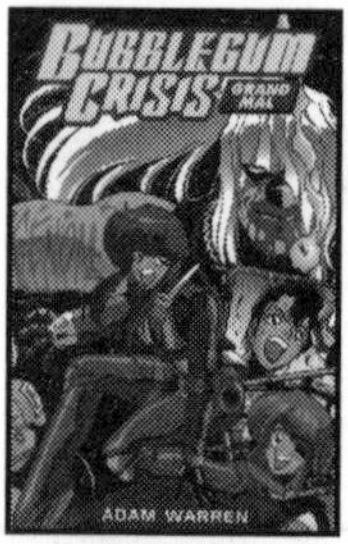
BUBBLEGUM CRISIS
GRAND MAL
ADAM WARREN

GRAND MAL
ISBN: 1-56971-120-8 $14.95

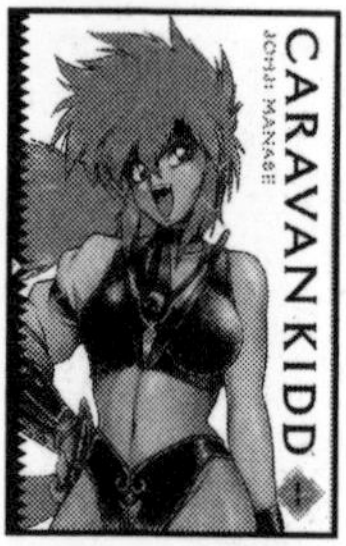
CARAVAN KIDD
JOHJI MANABE
1

VOLUME ONE
ISBN: 1-56971-260-3 $19.95

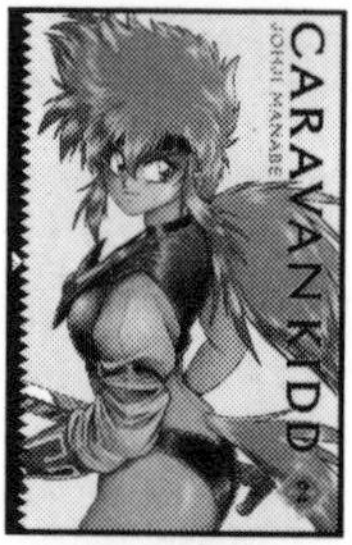
CARAVAN KIDD
JOHJI MANABE
2

VOLUME TWO
ISBN: 1-56971-324-3 $19.95

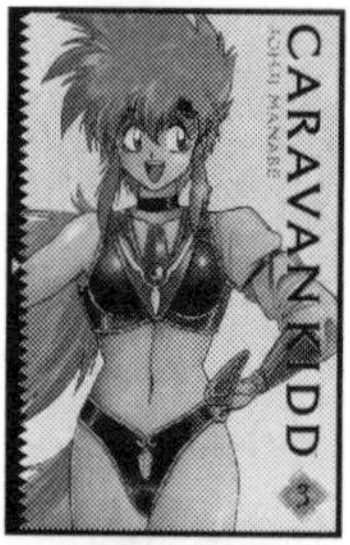
CARAVAN KIDD
JOHJI MANABE
3

VOLUME THREE
ISBN: 1-5-6971-338-3 $19.95

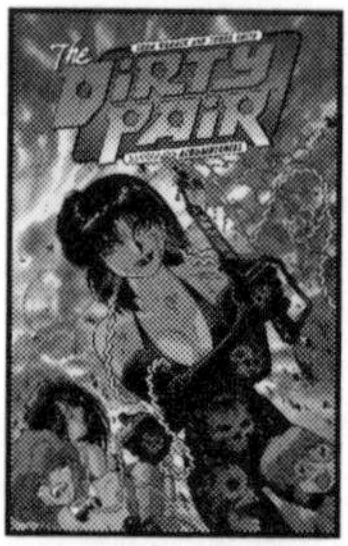
The Dirty Pair

DANGEROUS ACQUAINTANCES
ISBN: 1-56971-227-1 $12.95

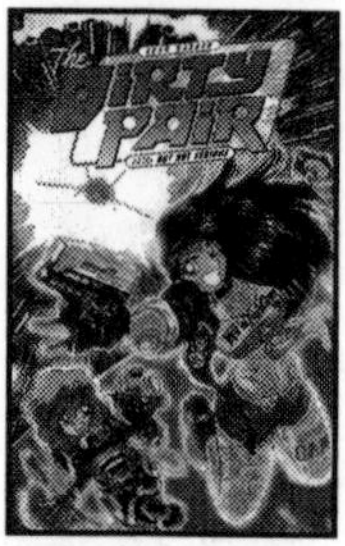
The Dirty Pair

FATAL BUT NOT SERIOUS
ISBN: 1-56971-172-0 $14.95

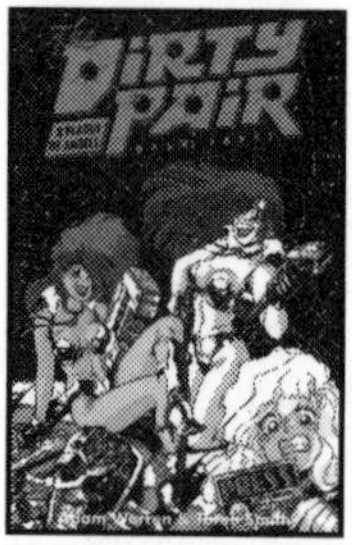
Dirty Pair

A PLAGUE OF ANGELS
ISBN: 1-56971-029-5 $12.95

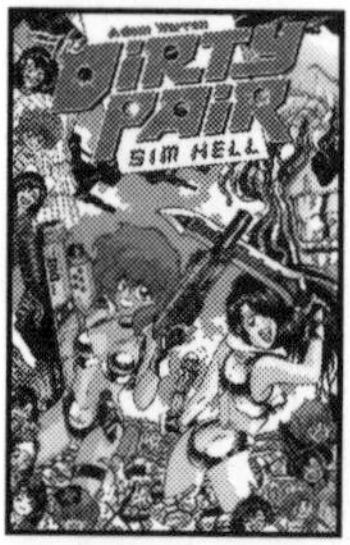
Adam Warren
The Dirty Pair
SIM HELL

SIM HELL
ISBN: 1-56971-159-3 $13.95

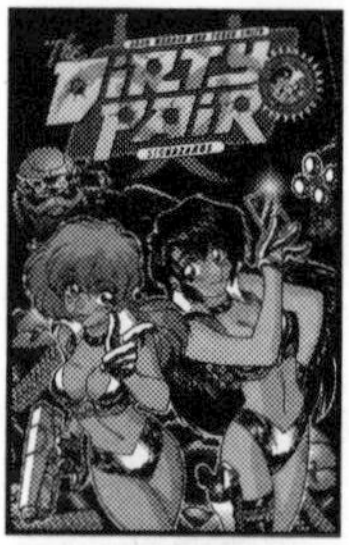
The Dirty Pair

BIOHAZARDS
ISBN:1-56917-339-1 $12.95

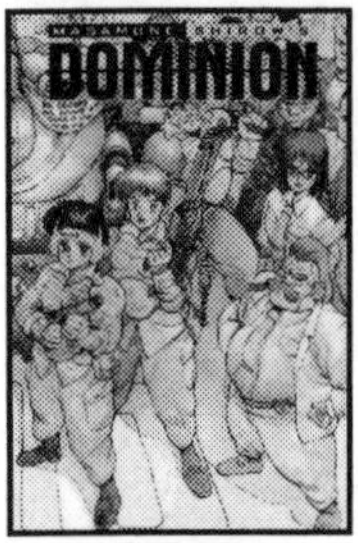
MASAMUNE SHIROW'S
DOMINION

DOMINION
ISBN: 1-56971-160-7 $14.95

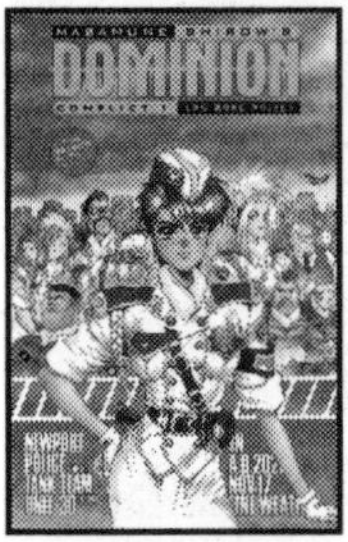
MASAMUNE SHIROW'S
DOMINION

CONFLICT 1: NO MORE NOISE
ISBN: 1-56971-233-6 $14.95

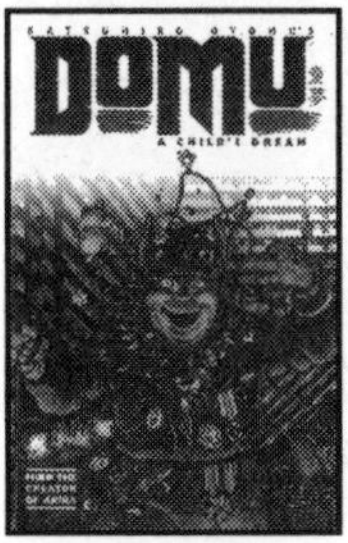
DOMU
A CHILD'S DREAM

A CHILD'S DREAM
ISBN: 1-56971-140-2 $17.95

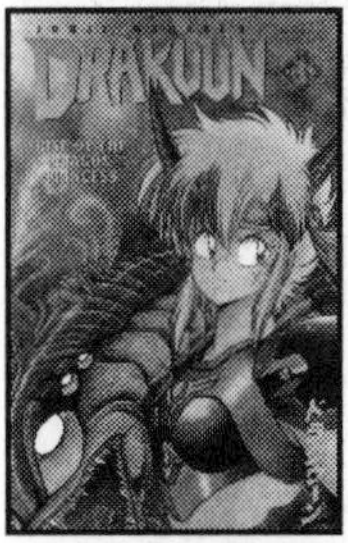
DRAKUUN

RISE OF THE DRAGON PRINCESS
ISBN: 1-56971-302-2 $12.95

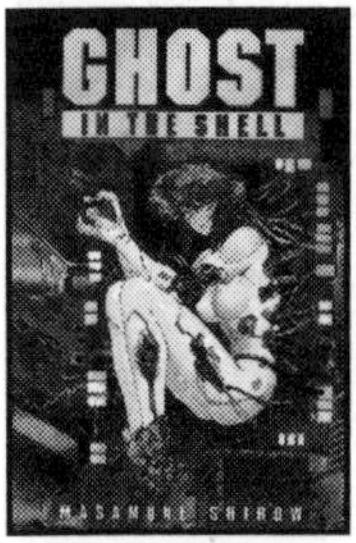
GHOST
IN THE SHELL
MASAMUNE SHIROW

GHOST IN THE SHELL
ISBN: 1-56971-081-3 $24.95

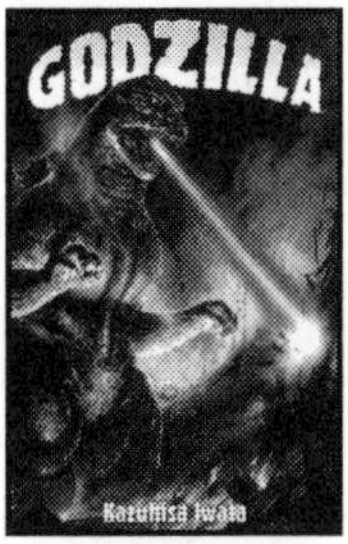
GODZILLA
Kazuhisa Iwata

GODZILLA
ISBN: 1-56971-063-5 $17.95

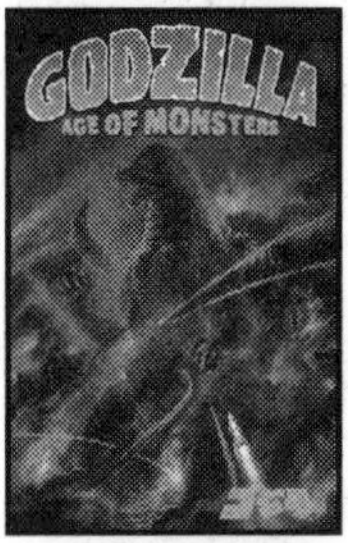
GODZILLA
AGE OF MONSTERS

AGE OF MONSTERS
ISBN: 1-56971-277-8 $17.95

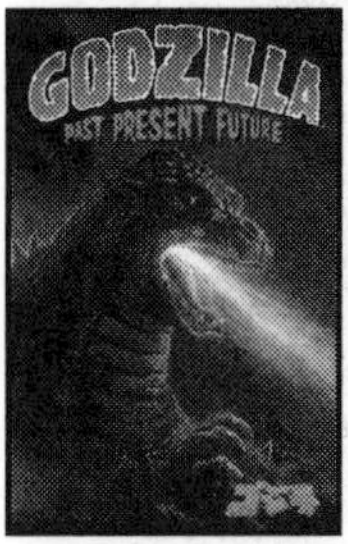
GODZILLA
PAST PRESENT FUTURE

PAST, PRESENT, AND FUTURE
ISBN: 1-56971-278-6 $17.95

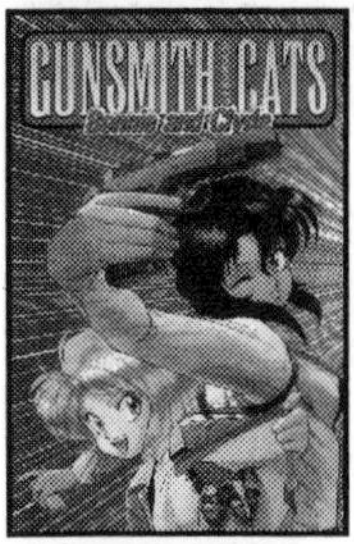
GUNSMITH CATS

BONNIE & CLYDE
ISBN: 1-56971-215-8 $13.95

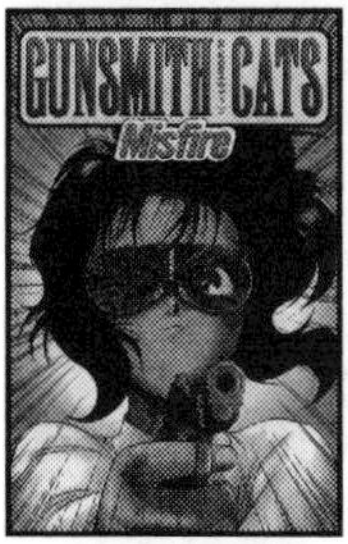
GUNSMITH CATS
Misfire

MISFIRE
ISBN: 1-56971-253-0 $12.95

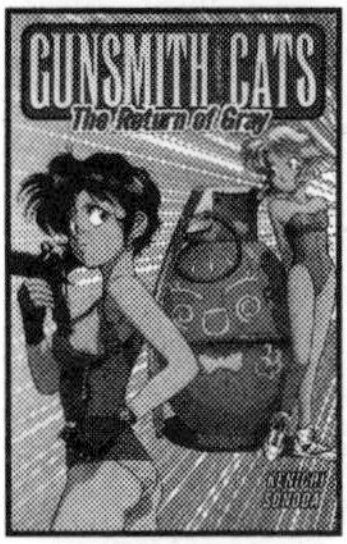
GUNSMITH CATS
The Return of Gray
KENICHI SONODA

RETURN OF GRAY
ISBN: 1-56971-299-9 $17.95

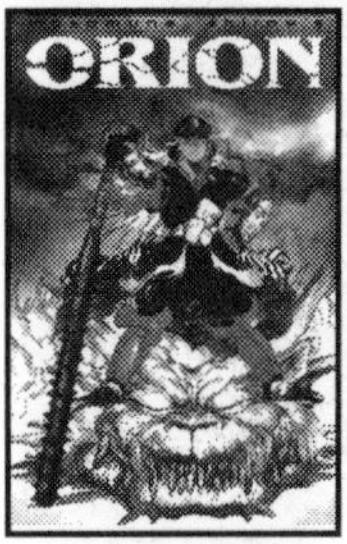
ORION

ORION
ISBN: 1-56971-148-8 $17.95

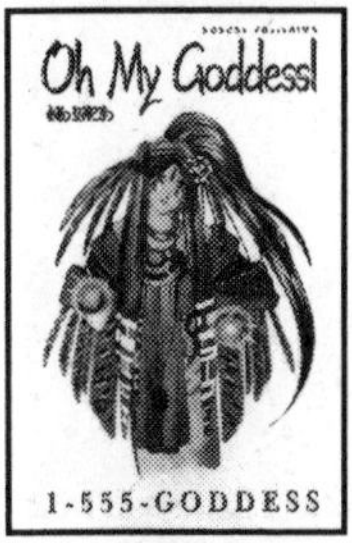
Oh My Goddess!
1-555-GODDESS

1-555-GODDESS
ISBN: 1-56971-207-7 $13.95

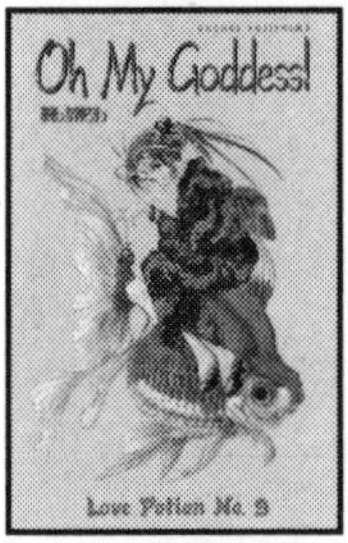
Oh My Goddess!
Love Potion No. 9

LOVE POTION NO. 9
ISBN: 1-56971-252-2 $12.95

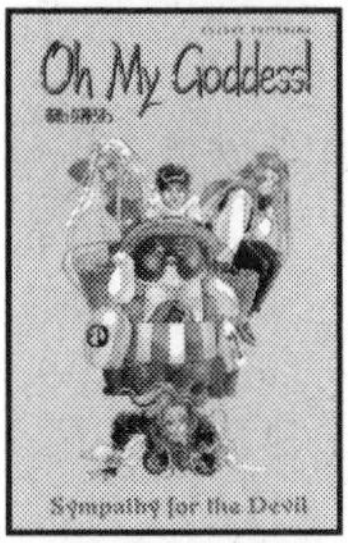
Oh My Goddess!
Sympathy for the Devil

SYMPATHY FOR THE DEVIL
ISBN: 1-56971-329-4 $12.95

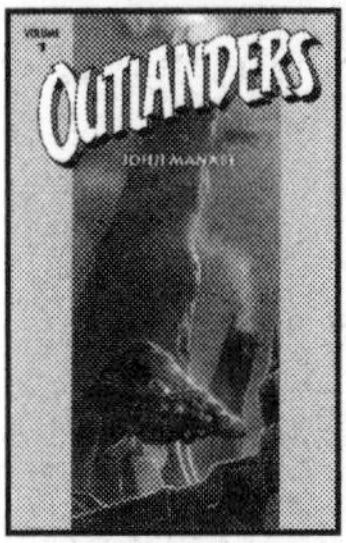
OUTLANDERS
JOHJI MANABE

VOLUME 1
ISBN: 1-56971-161-5 $13.95